New Nations and Peoples

Malaysia

Malaysia

VICTOR PURCELL

with 98 illustrations and 3 maps

New York
WALKER AND COMPANY

Contents

Preface

ON 16 SEPTEMBER 1963 THE FEDERATION OF MALAYSIA came into being, comprising the Federation of Malaya, Singapore, Sarawak and North Borneo which had hitherto been British Colonies. Its creation represented a daring political experiment since not only did it bring into close association for the first time territories which had been separately administered by the British in the past, but its establishment had been strongly opposed by Indonesia, and the Philippines had put forward claims to North Borneo, based on historical arguments. Indonesia adopted towards Malaysia a policy of 'confrontation', which apparently included every hostile measure short of war, and was manifested at once in the form of an economics boycott. But by 1966 peaceful relations had been restored between Malaysia and her two neighbours. Meanwhile, however – in 1965 – Singapore had seceded from Malaysia, and a period of tension opened up between the political leaderships of the two separate States.

Like other regions of the world, Southeast Asia has been divided into separate countries with very varying frontiers at different times. These boundaries have never exactly represented the divisions between peoples of different race or language, and have been drawn by a number of historical circumstances. The commonest factor was the conquest of territory by a single ruler, and, in recent times, by the establishment of the European colonial empires. The newly independent nations of Southeast Asia have indeed grown up from areas where the British, the Dutch, the French, and the Spanish succeeded by Americans had established their power. The Indonesians thus claimed West Irian (West New Guinea) on the ground

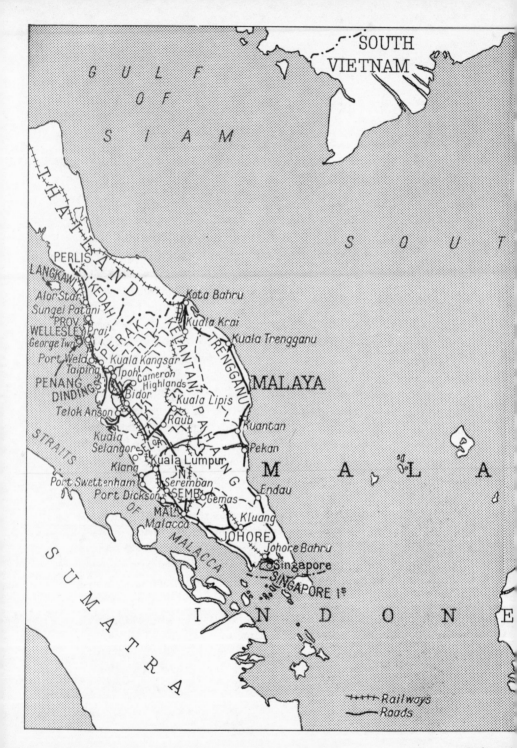

GULF

OF

SIAM

SOUTH
VIETNAM

S O U T

THAILAND

PERLIS

LANGKAWI

Alor Star

Sungei Patani

PROV.
WELLESLEY Prai

George Town

Port Weld

Taiping

PENANG
DINDINGS

Telok Anson

KEDAH

PERAK

Kuala Kangsar

Ipoh

Cameron
Highlands

Bidor

Kota Bahru

Kuala Krai

Kuala Trengganu

KELANTAN

TRENGGANU

MALAYA

Kuala Lipis

Raub

Kuala
Selangor

SELGR

Kuala Lumpur

Klang

Port Swettenham

Port Dickson

PAHANG

Kuantan

Pekan

M A L A

Endau

STRAITS

OF

MALACCA

NS.
Seremban

SEMB

MAL
Malacca

JOHORE

Gemas

Kluang

Johore Bahru

Singapore

SINGAPORE Is

SUMATRA

I N D O N E

+++++ Railways
——— Roads

Political

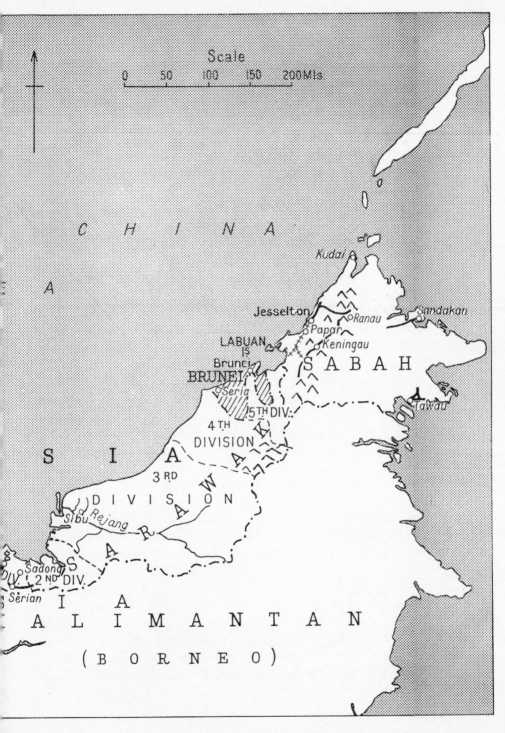

Malaysia

that it had once belonged to the Dutch East Indies – even though its inhabitants were of a completely different race from the other Indonesians.

Just as Indonesia took the place of Netherlands India, so Malaysia came into being in the region once ruled by the British. Its component units in the Malay Peninsula and in Borneo are separated by sea, and its racial make-up is diverse, but it nevertheless represents the fusion of important economic and strategical interests in accordance with the wishes of the great majority of its inhabitants.

The Federation of Malaysia comprises the Federation of Malaya (50,700 square miles), Sarawak (48,250 square miles), and Sabah (North Borneo) (29,388 square miles).

The capital is Kuala Lumpur, where the Parliament House is situated.

Malaya is a small country, elliptical in shape and almost nuzzling the equator (it lies between $1\frac{1}{2}°$ and $7°$ N), is about the size of England without Wales, and comprises eleven States – Perak, Selangor, Negri Sembilan, Pahang, Johore, Kedah, Kelantan, Trengganu, Perlis, Penang, and Malacca.

Before the Japanese occupation from 1941 to 1945, Malaya consisted of the British Colony of the Straits Settlements (Singapore, Penang, and Malacca), and of the British protected Malay States, four of them (Perak, Selangor, Negri Sembilan, and Pahang) being federated as the Federated Malay States (1896), and the remainder (Johore, Kedah, Kelantan, Trengganu, and Perlis) unfederated. Politically, Malaya was a unit solely through the fact that Britain was the Colonial Power (the Straits Settlements were British territory) and also the 'protecting Power', being in treaty relationship with the Malay states whereby each of its Rulers had undertaken to 'ask for and act upon British advice in all matters except those touching the Mohammedan religion and Malay custom'. The political co-ordination of these territories was secured through the fact that the Governor of the Straits Settlements was also High Commissioner for the Malay States, that North Borneo (now Sabah) and Brunei were under British protection (with the Governor of the Straits Settlements as High Commissioner), and that Christmas

Island in the Indian Ocean, producing phosphates (*not* the Christmas Island in the Pacific, which has in recent years been the scene of nuclear tests), was then administratively part of the Settlement of Singapore (in 1955 it was ceded to Australia).

During the period of the British Military Administration after the Japanese surrender (September 1945–April 1946) Malaya (including Singapore) was governed as a single unit, but, on the resumption of the civil government, a Malayan Union was created, comprising the Malay States of the mainland and the ex-Settlements of Penang and Malacca. Singapore remained British territory as a Colony. But, following upon widespread agitation among the Malays, the Union was, in February 1948, replaced by a Federation. The Malay Rulers of the states were given a leading place in it and the idea of complete amalgamation was suspended.

The Federation of Malaya became an independent sovereign state on 31 August 1957. Singapore was still a Colony but enjoyed internal self-government from 3 June 1959 onwards. With the creation of the Federation of Malaysia in August 1963, Singapore became independent as a unit of this Federation, enjoying autonomy in matters of labour and education and with a considerable measure of control over its own finances.

Sarawak was ruled for a century by the 'Three White Rajas' – from 1841 until the Japanese occupation of December 1941. The first of the three Rajas was Sir James Brooke who obtained the cession of the State from the Sultan of Brunei. Various accessions of territory were obtained between 1861 and 1905. In 1888 Sarawak was placed under British protection. After the liberation from the Japanese (1946), the last Raja, Sir Charles Vyner Brooke, who had resumed his rule, ceded the country to the British Crown and it became a Crown Colony.

North Borneo was a British protected state administered under a Royal Charter granted in 1881. The Sovereign rights and assets of the Company were transferred to the Crown with effect from 15 July 1946. On that date, the island of Labuan became part of the new Crown Colony of North Borneo.

Malaysia is not yet a 'nation', and although there is every hope that it may be welded into one in the future, it would be premature to survey it as a single unit. The plan of this book, therefore, is to give descriptions of Malaya, Sarawak, and Sabah (North Borneo) as well as Singapore now outside the Federation. In doing this, emphasis is placed on Malaya as being the 'key' unit of the Federation, and the account of Sarawak and Sabah is in less detail.

In writing this book, I have sought to emphasize the history and the natural, social, cultural, and economic aspects of the region. Politics, however, could not be ignored and I have discussed these in some detail in order to make the present situation intelligible. But in doing so, I hope that I have not obscured those factors that are enduring and which are likely to be as decisive in shaping the future of the region as they have been in shaping its past.

The name 'Malaysia' has been used in the past to describe the Malay Peninsula and Indonesia together. 'Malaysians' is used in the Census Reports of the Federation of Malaya and Singapore to include both Peninsular Malays and 'other Malaysians' – which means, in effect, Muslims from Sumatra, Java, etc., who had become absorbed into the local Malay population. In future it is likely that 'Malaysian' will be a term reserved for citizens of the Federation of Malaysia. The reader, meanwhile, should be warned against any confusion in nomenclature.

1   Malaya: Roots in the Past

THE HISTORY OF THE FAR EAST is not a mere record of vanished times; it is a guide to many of the happenings of the present day. In spite of the 'modernizing' that has been in process for the last few decades, institutions, customs, habits of thought, and even dress are still governed by tradition. The new 'nationalisms' are constantly appealing to the past, and, even when adopting revolutionary changes, seek to find the seeds of them in their own national histories. Thus while Communist China repudiates 'feudal' China as oppressive and reactionary, it points at the same time to ancient native institutions as the prototypes of its 'co-operatives', its State enterprises, and even its 'Communes'. Analogies are often stretched, and the 'past' evoked may on occasions be purely mythical, but it is essential in contemplating presentday Malaya to have in mind a coherent picture of the sequence of events over the last millennium. The study of history itself helps to create history.

Anthropology in recent times has received a powerful auxiliary in prehistory – 'the science', says Winstedt, 'of the cave, the cromlech, and the kitchen midden'. Together they have discovered and described the few places in the Far East where a pure palaeolithic culture existed; mainly in Mongolia along with Peking Man (*Sinanthropus*), in the terraces of the Solo River in Java, and at Kota Tampan near Lenggong in Upper Perak. At the latter spot in Malaya, in gravel beds overlaid by volcanic ash, primitive choppers have been found that may have been used by the earliest real 'men' of Peking and Java (*Homo modjokertensis* and *Pithecanthropus erectus*). Next comes a mesolithic culture of pebble tools. Artefacts belonging

13

to this culture are abundant in the caves and rock-shelters of the limestone cliffs in the north and centre of the Malay Peninsula, and the race that used them must have inhabited it for several thousand years until between 2500 and 1500 B.C. when they were driven south by makers of a more efficient tool – the 'polished neolith'. These mesoliths were probably related to the modern Australian aborigine and the Melanesians of New Caledonia and the Loyalty Islands.

Then came the Bronze Age. The Peninsula's most important relics of the Bronze Age are two kettledrums – one revealed by a flood in Pahang and the other dug up in Selangor by the Japanese in 1944. Some of Malaya's aboriginal people, still extant, the Negritos and the Senoi, are associated with those primitive cultures, which, in turn, were succeeded by a Bronze–Iron Age whose remains are bronze relics and iron tools. The Proto-Malays of this period are still to be found in Malaya. Their ancestors domesticated cattle and probably irrigated rice-fields. They practised, too, a shamanism destined to be profoundly affected by the Indian type with its belief in spirit-possession.

The racial make-up of the Malaysians and of their neighbours in Southeast Asia is extremely mixed. The region has been called an 'ethnographical museum'. In Sumatra, for example, there are long-headed Caucasoids (Nesiots) represented by the Bataks, and the broad-headed Mongoloid type which emigrated hither from Continental Asia via Malaya and which is found daily in Sumatra's East Coast. Malaya also has a diversity of peoples, and it would be a mistake to imagine that they have not to some extent intermarried over the centuries. The 'Proto-Malays' (*Jakun*), too, are of the same stock as the Malays proper, and in certain areas are so absorbed into the ordinary Malay community as not to be separately distinguished. Nevertheless, in spite of the different racial strains among them, the 'Malaysians' are to the eye, remarkably homogeneous. Whereas there is an obvious difference between the Melanesians of New Guinea and the peoples of Indonesia, Southeast Asians from Burma to Lombok and Vietnam to Acheh give the impression of being of common stock. The 'Malaysians' are further from the Chinese, but not so very much further, since like them they are 'Mongoloid'. The barrier to intermarriage between Malays and Chinese is not 'racial', but religious and social.

Long before the Chinese–Indian influences were extended to South-east Asia, the great prehistoric migrations had ended. In the Indonesian islands, the peoples who had established themselves there in Neolithic times were divided already into the 'Malays' of many admixtures of the coasts and the races who had retained their purity of race to a greater extent – for example, the Bataks of Sumatra, the Dayaks of Borneo, and the Alfurs of the Celebes and the Moluccas.

Malay contact with India probably antedated the Christian era by some centuries, but about the beginning of that era Indians arrived in Southeast Asia in greater numbers – among them priests or monks who brought a calendar, the art of writing, and new ideas on law and administration. Sometimes a Malay chief would be admitted to the warrior caste of *Kshatriyas*, adopting Hinduism; those Indians who married into the families of local chiefs brought Hindu ideas of kingship, just as more than a thousand years later Muslim Tamils married into the families of Malay rulers and prime ministers (*Bendahara*) of Malacca; but Hindu and Buddhist contacts at first hardly extended beyond courts and ports. The influence was Indian, but the culture of Malaya was indigenous. The peasant of the interior still remained an animist and an ancestor-worshipper with a mythology of his own.

The first Indianized Kingdom in Malaya was Langkasuka. This is the 'Lang-ya-hsiu' of the Chinese history of the Liang dynasty (A.D. 502–56), which says that the state had been founded in the second century, had walled towns and produced aloe-wood and camphor oil. Its people had long hair and went bare to the waist and wore a cotton skirt while the king and his nobles affected thin flowered shawls, gold girdles, and gold earrings. The king went abroad on an elephant, seated under a white *howdah* and escorted by soldiers, drummers, and followers carrying fans and banners (it needed the pragmatic pen of the Chinese historian to lend actuality to events for the first time: the Indians were too transcendental to record such mundane trivialities). Archaeological remains testify to Indianized settlements in what are now the states of Kedah and Perak as early as the fourth century A.D. The earliest traders of historical times were from the Coromandel coast, the county of the Pallavas. Those Southern Indians were devotees of Brahma, Vishnu, and Siva, but Buddhist inscriptions are extant in Kedah and Province Wellesley, testifying also to the arrival of India's great 'Hindu Protestantism' – the Buddhist religion.

Other important civilizations under India's influence had arisen and declined in Indo-China at an early time, but the first great power to include Malaya definitely within its sway was the Buddhist empire of Sri Vijaya.

Sri Vijaya figures prominently in the mystique of Indonesian nationalism, but it must not be forgotten that its existence is a modern rediscovery. As recently as 1908 an authority on ancient Java, Dr Kern, mistook Sri Vijaya for the name of a person ('Sri' is a Sanskrit honorific both for persons and places). It was the distin-guished French historian of Southeast Asia, Coedès, who first revealed it as the important empire it actually was. It had its begin-ning at Palembang in the south of Sumatra in the seventh century A.D. In 686 it carried out a successful expedition against Java, and by 775 it had obtained a footing in Ligor in north Malaya. In the world of commerce, Sri Vijaya (now called San-fo-ts'i by the Chinese and Zabag [=Sumatra] by the Arabs), had extended its control over both the Straits of Sunda and the Straits of Malacca. About A.D. 850 Sri Vijaya was inherited by one of the Sailendra, a dynasty of kings famous as patrons of Javanese music and the builders of those great examples of Buddhist architecture, the temple of Tara at Kalasan, Chandit Mendut, and the world famous Borobodur. In 863 they lost their Javanese kingdom to Hindu rivals. Much of the mystique of modern Southeast Asian nationalism is built up on exaggeration or pure myth, but Borobodur is a splendid achievement of art and the expression of a highly sophisticated civilization.

A few facts suggest the range of Sri Vijaya's grip on the Malay Peninsula. From a mine at Bidor in Perak there was dredged up a fine eight-armed Mahayana bronze of about the tenth century A.D., representing the Bodhisattva Avalo-Kitesvara (metamorphosed into a woman as the Chinese Kuan Yin, or Goddess of Mercy), and at open-cast mines at Sungei Siput two other fine Buddhist bronzes. A Chinese map of 1584, copied from an older chart, puts San-fo-ts'i in the middle of the Malay Peninsula. And Tomé Pires, writing about 1512, tells how Kedah in the middle of the fifteenth century still claimed tribute from Perak, Manjong, Bernam, Selangor, and Malacca, obviously as Sri Vijaya's local heir.

At length, however, Sri Vijaya decayed before raids from Chola or Coromandel, on the east coast of India. For long the battle was a ding-dong one, and Sri Vijaya continued to send envoys to China, taking camphor, silver, and pearls as a tribute, receiving presents and titles in return, and buying golden girdles and purple robes for Buddhist monks. By 1071 many of Sri Vijaya's subject territories were independent. Though the centre lingered on in Sumatra, so far as can be gathered from scattered inscriptions, the glory of Sri Vijaya, a Venice of the East, had passed.

Singosari arose in East Java, and it represents a further stage in the evolution of Hindu-Javanese culture. Under the great warrior king, Kertanagara (1268–92), it reached out to seize the dominions of Sri Vijaya, which continued to hold out in its Sumatran capital though encircled by its Javanese enemies. It was Kertanagara, too, whose temerity caused the appearance of a Chinese fleet and army on the Javanese scene. When ambassadors from Kublai Khan, the Mongol Emperor of China (1260–94), appeared at Singosari in 1289, Kertanagara at once seized them and expelled them with ignominy. The result was that in 1292 the Mongol emperor dis-patched a punitive expedition to Java. When it arrived the situation had changed, Kertanagara had been murdered and replaced by a usurper, one Jayakatwang. The son-in-law of Kertanagara, the previous Crown Prince Vijaya, now joined forces with the Chinese and together they easily overthrew Jayakatwang. Vijaya had promised to recognize Kublai Khan's overlordship over Java, but

17

as soon as the usurper was disposed of Vijaya turned on the Chinese and after a series of surprise attacks he forced them to re-embark the remains of their army and to head back to China. Vijaya thereupon founded a new dynasty, the Majapahit, the last of the Hindu-Javanese Kingdoms. (It is episodes such as these, the triumph of the native people over the intruding foreigner, which capture the imagination of modern Southeast Asian schoolchildren – though this particular episode belongs rather to Indonesian than to Malay nationalism.)

Some time between 1335 and 1365, Java's new empire, Majapahit, conquered Jambi, Palembang, and Minangkabau – in effect all Sumatra. Palembang passed into the hands of the Chinese under Cantonese leadership, and though they mostly existed by piracy, they were able to maintain their independence there for nearly two hundred years.

Majapahit, like Sri Vijaya, was a Hindu empire. It claimed suzerainty over the Riau Archipelago, the Anambas, and the Natunal Islands and also subjected Sri Vijaya's colonies in the Malay Peninsula. Majapahit's great days of expansion were the middle years of the fourteenth century. At its greatest extent, this last of the Hindu-Javanese empires held dominion over part of Sumatra and the Malay Peninsula as far north as Kedah, Langkasuka, and Patani, over the fringe of the south and west coast of Borneo, and over Southern Celebes and the Moluccas. It even claimed a protec-torate over the countries of the Indo-Chinese peninsula. But its actual control was limited to Java, and it did not emulate the cultural achievement of its predecessor. On the whole it was content to sack without colonizing. Its most notable king, Hayam Wuruk, was a conqueror rather than a statesman.

Tumasik, or old Singapore, though less important than the Malay kingdoms that lay to the north, has been given a glamour and a prominence by the folk-tales in the *Malay Annals* and because it later became the seat of Parameswara, the founder of the Kingdom of Malacca, the ancestor of most of the sultanates of twentieth-century Malaya. Its history is shadowy and the facts confused, and the one great chance of sorting them out was lost when the stele with an inscription in Majapahit characters that stood at the mouth of the Singapore river was blown up by the Public Works Department in course of road construction (an act of vandalism which that other wise creative department was never allowed to forget).

Parameswara (a title meaning 'prince-consort') was, it seems, a prince of Palembang who had married a princess of Majapahit. At some point he announced his independence of Majapahit – which proved a rash step, for a Javanese expedition thereupon attacked him in Palembang and forced him to flee. In his flight he found refuge in the island of Tumasik, or Singapore. This was about 1390.

Although welcomed by the reigning chief of Tumasik (perhaps through *force majeure*), Parameswara (according to the account of Tomé Pires, d'Albuquerque's druggist) had him murdered within eight days of his arrival, claiming the island and the neighbouring sea-passages as his own. But his position was insecure, since the murdered chief had been related both to the King of Siam and the ruler of Patani, a vassal state to Siam. Nevertheless, Tomé Pires says, he remained for five years in Singapore. However, on the news of the approach of a belated avenging war fleet from Patani, Parameswara decided that it would be wise to start on his travels again and embarked with his followers.

Parameswara's next place of residence was Muar (in modern Johore) where he established a settlement and for some six years or so he and his subjects lived by fishing, farming, and piracy. He then moved northward to what appeared to be a more promising place of settlement, namely Malacca, then only a village, for here was a combination of river, hill, and flat land which offered possibilities for trade, agriculture, and defence. This was probably about A.D. 1400.[1]

The beginnings of the Kingdom of Malacca were very modest, but some three years after his arrival, Parameswara was brought to the centre of a series of dramatic happenings which signalized Ming China's burst of maritime adventure between 1403 and 1431.

In 1403, says the Ming History, the Emperor of China sent a eunuch Yin Ching as envoy to Malacca with presents of silk brocade. By this time Malacca had become feudatory to Siam. The King Pa٬li٬su٬ra (Parameswara), says the history, 'was very glad' and in 1405 sent a return mission to China. The emperor spoke in laudatory terms of their master, appointed him king of the country of Malacca, and gave him a commission, a seal, a suit of silk clothes, and a yellow umbrella. The king, through his representatives, then 'requested that the mountains might be made guardians of the country, to which request the emperor gave his consent; he prepared an inscription with a piece of verse at the end, and ordered a tablet to be erected to those mountains'. In 1407 Parameswara again sent envoys to China.

But the more noteworthy event of the era was the arrival in 1409 of the Chinese admiral, Cheng Ho, later deified by the Overseas Chinese as Sam Po Kung. Cheng (like Yin Ching) had been a eunuch at the court of the third Ming emperor of the Ming (of the Yung Lo reign). Arising out of Cheng Ho's visit, Parameswara again visited China in 1411 with his wife, his son, his ministers, and attendants – altogether 450 persons. They were lodged in the Board of Rites, received in audience by the emperor, and entertained on a grand scale. They were presented with gifts of precious stones, horses and saddles, 100 ounces of gold, 500 ounces of silver, and 400,000 *kwan* of paper money. On their way back officers entertained them at two different stations on the road. In the same year the King of Malacca's nephew came to return thanks for this hospitality.

The voyages of Cheng Ho and his fellow admirals continued at intervals until 1431, then suddenly ceased, never to be resumed by the Chinese. In the course of them the Chinese penetrated to the coast of Africa and the Persian gulf and Mecca was visited by members of the expeditions. Fleets are described of sixty٬two vessels carrying 37,000 soldiers. Chiefs and kings were deposed, like those of Palembang and Ceylon, and sent as captives to China. The voyages ceased as suddenly as they had begun, and the reasons seem to have been political, following the gaining of power by the party opposed to adventures abroad. But Malacca continued to send tribute to China notwithstanding.

These Ming voyages still have a significance in the modern

political scene. The loose suzerainty established by China at this time over most of the countries of Southeast Asia and beyond lends colour to the suggestion that Communist China is 'expansionist' and has ambitions to restore the Ming overseas 'empire'. But positive evidence of this 'expansionism' has, so far, not been produced.

While these events were happening, Majapahit was still extant, though the forces destined to overwhelm it were now assembling. In the north the Thai Kingdom of Siam (as it became known to the Portuguese), centred since 1350 in the Menam delta, was emerging as the most powerful state of the Indo-Chinese peninsula, and increasingly put forward claims to suzerainty farther south which conflicted with those of Majapahit. In the south, the growing commercial prosperity of ports such as Melayu (Jambi) in Sumatra was encouraging them to assert their independence. But it was the rise of Islam, closely associated with commerce, which had already taken root in the coastal states of Sumatra and was beginning to fan westwards across the Malay Peninsula and the Indonesian islands, that foreshadowed the doom of the Hindu Kingdom of Majapahit. It is surprising, indeed, that in spite of the irresistible advance of Islam the empire lingered on so long. The facts of its actual collapse are obscure but the Dutch historian, Krom, is of the opinion that it finally fell between 1513 and 1528 before a coalition of Muslim states composed of Madura, Tuban, Surabaya, and Bintara (Demak).

Like Hinduism and Buddhism, which had preceded it in Southeast Asia by many centuries, Islam made its first impacts in the royal courts; only later, and very gradually, did it spread to the mass of the people. The path of Islam to Southeast Asia lay via India, and Indian Muslims played a very prominent part in its diffusion. The first Muslim states were established in northern Sumatra towards the end of the thirteenth century, and it was through marriage to a princess of one of these states, Pasai, that the first King of Malacca, Parameswara, adopted the Muslim religion at his court in 1414. How far Islam was the religion of the second king, Sri Maharaja, is debatable, but the accession of Muzaffar Shah, following the palace revolution of 1445, ensured a Muslim succession.

21

But the spread of Islam among the people of Malacca did not mean the end of Hinduism. Hindu influences were still detectable among the Malays of the 1960s. Their literature is full of Sanskrit words for abstract things such as *danger, intellect, kindness, language, name, profit, property, religion, heaven* and *hell*. The shadow-play, which is still to be witnessed in the East Coast states, is of Hindu origin. Hindu traditions linger, too, in the court ceremonial and Sanskrit words are used for titles of rank (e.g. *Bendahara, Laksamana,* etc.), and announcements in Sanskrit are made at the royal investitures. Above all it was the influence of the Hindu religion which softened the impact of Islam and made the Malays unfanatical in their devotion to Mohammed and their worship of Allah.

While Islam was establishing its hold on Malacca and Muslim theologians flocked to the port, the kingdom was prospering. As the history of the Malays emerges from the timeless fables of the *Malay Annals*, rulers and people assume a more material roundness and a definite extension in time and space. The port was now attracting a tremendous variety of trade and traders from India, China, and the kingdoms of Southeast Asia. The *Malay Annals* give us glimpses of the development of law and the protection of merchants' property. Large ships anchored just south of the Malacca river estuary (it was the silting up of the harbour which eventually crippled Malacca as a port) and small craft swarmed in the river itself. A complex system of trade routes led to Malacca from both east and west, trade from the Red Sea and the Persian Gulf joining up with that coming from the Mediterranean. During the trading seasons, governed by the monsoons, Malacca was a huge fairground where the products of many centres were exchanged – Venetian glass and metal ware, and Arabian opium, perfumes, pearls, dyes, cloths, tapestries and incense came in with the south-west monsoon from April to October; spices, porcelain, damasks, silks, gold and tin, even birds from the Banda Islands whose feathers had a market in Arabia and Turkey sailed out with the north-east monsoon from October to April.

From the judicious taxation of the trade, the Sultans of Malacca grew rich and powerful, and possessing riches and power they were no longer willing to play second fiddle to rulers of other states. Muzzafar Shah, the first ruler of Malacca to use the title of Sultan (in 1445), refused to send tribute to Siam. Thereupon a Siamese army, dispatched to Malacca by the difficult overland route via Pahang, was defeated and withdrew. The defeat of a second Siamese invasion in 1456 marked a turning-point in Malacca's history. Hitherto it had built up its resources, but it now embarked on a policy reminiscent of those of Sri Vijaya. Expeditions sent across the Straits of Malacca conquered Siak and Kampar in Indragiri and Rokan. The small states of the Malay Peninsula from Kedah to Johore and the Riau Archipelago were compelled to make their deference to Malacca's supremacy.

We are on the eve, now, of what in the centuries to come was to have revolutionary consequences to Malaya and the whole of Asia – namely the arrival of the Europeans in military array. For long, however, the impression they made on Asia was slight. It was only after the Scientific Renaissance had taken place in Europe from the sixteenth century onwards, producing in turn the Industrial Revolution, that Europe began to conquer Asia and to administer a large portion of it. Before then, the Portuguese, the Dutch, and the English were in Asia on sufferance, maintaining their outposts by a combination of sea power and diplomacy.

The first arrivals in this new 'drive to the East' were the Portuguese, adventurers from a small country on the Atlantic seaboard. They came, they declared, for 'Christians and spices', by which they meant to convert the infidel at the point of the sword and to line their pockets in doing it. Having waged war for generations to secure their independence from the Moors, they now came to gain direct access to the spice trade, hitherto monopolized by the co-religionists of the Moors, the Arabs, who used the Venetians as their European agents.

In no person was the bellicosity and the vaulting ambition of the still half-savage Portuguese more completely embodied than in the person of Affonso d'Albuquerque, the second Governor-General of the Indies. A single episode will suffice to illustrate this. D'Albuquerque conceived two projects to bring discomfort to

Portugal's arch enemies, the 'Moors' – the first was to dig a canal from the Red Sea to the Nile and so draw off the waters of the Nile delta, thus desiccating Egypt's fields, the second was to land an expeditionary force to seize the body of the Prophet at Medina and to hold it to ransom. Both these projects were serious ones and d'Albuquerque actually indented on Lisbon for Portuguese miners from Madeira to cut the canal! But not all d'Albuquerque's projects were as visionary as these. Having established a line of ports in India, d'Albuquerque resolved to strike at the very heart of the 'Moorish' spice trade and to capture Malacca.

Two hours before dawn on 6 June 1511, the day sacred to the Apostle James, a trumpet sounded on d'Albuquerque's flagship, in the van of his fleet drawn up before Malacca. Captains and men-at-arms assembled on the flagship's deck, and bared their heads in confession. Then with the rising of the sun the assault began. But it was to prove no easy victory. Again and again the Portuguese were driven back by the Malays manning the stockades. The sultan and his sons, mounted on elephants, directed the defence until, pricked by the attacking lances, the elephants swung round and charged the 'Moors'' own ranks. Malacca's storehouse of fragrant spices was now on fire and burning fiercely. Mortally wounded, the elephant bearing Ahmad, the sultan's son, killed its *mahout*, but Ahmad, though wounded himself, escaped in the confusion.

But the fight was not yet over, and it was only after successive attacks over nine whole days, some of which ended in disaster, that the town was carried. Then, to clear the streets and the bombards from the house-tops, no quarter was given to man, woman, or child and there ensued a hecatomb of butchery. The conquest of Malacca was remarkable for the gallant and determined defence offered by the Malays but it was even more remarkable for the tenacious ferocity of the Portuguese attack, since they were much fewer in numbers.

The Portuguese held Malacca from 1511 to 1641. All ships passing through the Straits were required to call at Malacca and pay the appropriate duties. In default of compliance, the Portuguese patrols took drastic measures and, in addition, large presents were extracted from foreign traders. This high-handed action tended in time to cause the trade to seek other ports. The Portuguese from Malacca established posts in the Moluccas or elsewhere in the islands. Pressing on to China, they were eventually allowed by the Chinese to maintain a station (under the supervision of a Chinese mandarin) at Macao.

Since theirs was a small nation unable to colonize on any great scale, the Portuguese sought the perpetuation of their name and culture by intermarriage with the indigenous peoples. Although this policy increased the number of Christians in Malacca (to 7,400 in 1613, says Eredia) it did not succeed in establishing Portuguese power on a stable basis. To this day, however, the majority of the small Eurasian community in Malaya is of Portuguese descent.

During its career of 130 years, the Portuguese settlement was often on the defensive. Between 1515-24, and again in 1551 and 1616, there were serious Johore attacks on the fortress, and that of 1551 seems to have come very near to success. At times the Portuguese counter-attacked vigorously, as in 1526 when they destroyed the Johore capital on the island of Bintang, but the Portuguese hold was always precarious – they never established an 'empire' in the real sense of the word.

It cannot be said that Portuguese culture was a higher one than that of the Malays. The Europeans did introduce some refinements of the table and the house, as is suggested by a number of Malay words – *keju* (cheese), *mantega* (butter), *almeirah* (wardrobe). But a far greater number of words for sophisticated things came from Arabic or Persian – *seluar* (trousers) and *baju* (coat) are both of Persian origin. Altogether the Portuguese imprint on Malaya was superficial.

The European successors to the Portuguese in many of their Asian possessions were the Dutch. They were of quite a different type. Feeling no need to proselytize (their own salvation being assured by their Calvinistic creed), they did not dissipate their energies on missionary activity but concentrated on a single objective – trade. Their policy, as formulated by Jan Pieterszoon Coen (d. 1629) was to control all Asian trade by means of sea power and to levy toll on it. This was feasible only so long as the Dutch retained control of the seas, and when they lost this to the English towards the end of the seventeenth century the East Indian Company had increasingly to rely on the growing of produce (sugar, coffee, spices). Their rivalry with the Portuguese caused them to plan to capture Malacca, and this, after several repulses, they were finally able to accomplish in 1641. But the Portuguese commander withstood the siege for months and did not surrender until the garrison was starving (he did *not* sell the fort to the Dutch as is stated by Karl Marx in *Capital*). The operation was a combined one between the Dutch and Johore who were now in alliance.

Dutch Malacca was mainly a fortress from which the Dutch trading interests could be watched in the Straits. Only in a very subordinate sense was it a centre of trade. Like the Portuguese, the Dutch were monopolistic – they claimed the right to tax exports and imports of every commodity within the reach of their strong right arm. Batavia (hitherto named Jakarta, and Jakarta or Djakarta it is once more since Indonesian independence) remained the main entrepôt and Malacca was only the outpost.

The Dutch sought by means of treaties with the local rulers to secure exclusive trading privileges in the purchase of spices, gold, pepper and tin. By becoming sole purchasers, the Dutch could also hope to become the sole distributors, notably of Indian textiles, which were supplied from their own depots in India. Actually the treaties (often made under pressure) were difficult to enforce; there was competition from the Bugis of the Celebes and Indian Muslim traders were able to secure tin and other Straits' produce from ports in the Straits. But the Dutch persevered, their patrols policing the Straits and forcing passing ships to call in at Malacca to pay their taxes and to obtain permits to continue their voyage. Needless to say, this coercive policy inhibited the growth of trade. The population of Malacca remained small throughout Dutch times. In 1795 the settlement was occupied by the British in the name of the Prince of Orange, was returned to the Dutch in 1818 by the terms of the Treaty of Vienna, and was finally ceded by them to Britain in return for Bencoolen in Sumatra, by the Anglo–Dutch treaty of 1824.

Mahmud, the last King of Malacca, fled from the Portuguese, first to Johore and then to Pahang, seeking refuge with a prince who had hitherto been his vassal. Hoping that a counter-attack might regain his kingdom for him, he appealed to the Emperor of China for help, but without result. After less than a year's residence in Pahang, Mahmud left to seek a new home in Johore. The site he chose was Bintang, to the south-east of Singapore. Having lost one kingdom, he (or perhaps his son Alauddin) was to become the founder of another.

From Johore, Mahmud launched attacks on Malacca (1515, 1519, 1523, 1524) which were repulsed by the Portuguese, who in return raided Johore as a reprisal. They captured and then in 1526 destroyed Bintang, and Mahmud was once again in exile, fleeing this time to Kampar in Sumatra where he died two years later. For more than a hundred years the history of Johore was punctuated with the names of new capitals from which new sultans were expelled to die in exile. Not only the Portuguese, but neighbouring states such as Acheh, conducted these devastating attacks. Yet Johore survived to make its terms with the Dutch and to become their ally.

A Dutch–Johore agreement was made in 1637, and in 1641 Johore, as we have seen, assisted the Dutch in their capture of Malacca. Perhaps the best advantage that Johore obtained from the alliance was to be left alone to build up its own trade in the Johore river valley. 'Never (says Winstedt) had any period in Johore history opened with brighter prospects.' The Portuguese power was broken; the Dutch at Malacca were friendly, and they were long to remain on peaceful terms. Acheh, too, had ceased to be a threat. Under Sultan Abdul Jalil Shah II (1623–77), with new alliances with Patani and Jambi in Sumatra, Johore seemed on the way to repeat the 'success story' of Malay Malacca.

But there came a series of unhappy events which finally destroyed the whole structure of the empire. The first was the long war with Jambi (1666–86). In 1717, a Siak prince, Kechil, led a Minang-kabau force into Johore and deposed the sultan. Then the Bugis came on the scene to impose their yoke on Johore; furthermore they made an attack on Malacca, which was followed by a counter-attack on Lingga. In 1750 the Bugis accepted peace terms whereby they acknowledged the lawful sovereignty of the Sultans of Johore and confirmed the Dutch claims to a monopoly of the tin trade. But this was merely an interlude: after an interval the Bugis re-established their control. First of all the Minangkabaus, and then the Bugis and the Dutch had destroyed whatever chance there was of holding a Johore empire together.

There is, in retrospect, nothing particularly impressive in this Malay attempt to re-create the glories of the Malacca sultanate. Malacca in the fifteenth century had been a queen in her own right, representing a culture which was an amalgam of Hindu, Arab, and Persian influences with the basic Malay society. But now that the Europeans had arrived, the technical civilization they represented was developing in power year by year with the impulse of the Scientific Renaissance in Europe. The Malays, therefore, were fighting a losing battle with the West, though they realized the truth only by degrees.

What alienates the reader from this particular period is the quality of despotism and a cruel capriciousness without grandeur. This is illustrated by the story of Mahmud who succeeded to the throne of Johore in 1683. Having been presented with a pair of handsome English pistols by the adventurer, Alexander Hamilton, he tried them out by shooting the first of his Malay subjects he happened to meet outside the palace. The notion of princely or aristocratic pre-rogative independent of responsibility, however, was characteristic of Malay society not only at this period but in the nineteenth century as well.

The Bugis' influence on Malaya was largely destructive. They weakened the Malay Sultanate of Johore beyond repair; they helped to weaken Malay authority in Kedah and Perak. At the same time they created a new state and dynasty in Selangor which has lasted to the present day. They also kept the Dutch in check, competing with them for the spice trade, and prevented the extension of their power. In the end they were merged into the general Malay population. Altogether, with its fragmentation and its petty wars and feuds, the Malay world was in no way organized to oppose the forces that were to be arrayed against it in the nineteenth century. European power was increasing. The British Empire in India was consolidating and this involved almost inevitably an extension into Southeast Asia if only for the safeguarding of its frontiers. The growth of the British trade with China (especially in tea) would demand a chain of stations to keep open the way thither. The Dutch, after the Treaty of Vienna, were re-established in the East Indies and were jealous trade rivals of the British. How were the petty Malay states of the Peninsula to survive the advance of those two giants? But although the die was cast, it was to be many years before the tide of European colonization, or 'imperialism', starting perhaps as a tiny trickle in the laboratory of a Boyle or the study of a Newton (rather than in the barrack-square of a Marlborough), would begin to lap round the principalities of Malaya. This 'imperialism' was in essence the expression of a technological superiority increasingly possessed by the West and reversing a trend which, up to the Middle Ages, had been in the opposite direction.[2]

I This bronze representation of the Bodhisattva Avalo-Kitesvara is a relic of the Buddhist empire of Sri Vijaya which originated in south Sumatra in the seventh century A.D. and was the first great Power to bring Malaya within its sway.

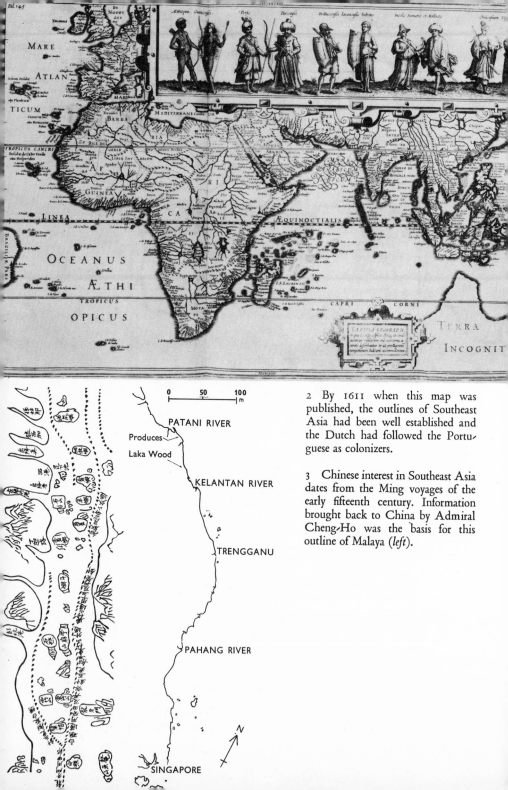

PATANI RIVER

Produces
Laka Wood

KELANTAN RIVER

TRENGGANU

PAHANG RIVER

SINGAPORE

0 50 100 m

N

2 By 1611 when this map was published, the outlines of Southeast Asia had been well established and the Dutch had followed the Portuguese as colonizers.

3 Chinese interest in Southeast Asia dates from the Ming voyages of the early fifteenth century. Information brought back to China by Admiral Cheng-Ho was the basis for this outline of Malaya (*left*).

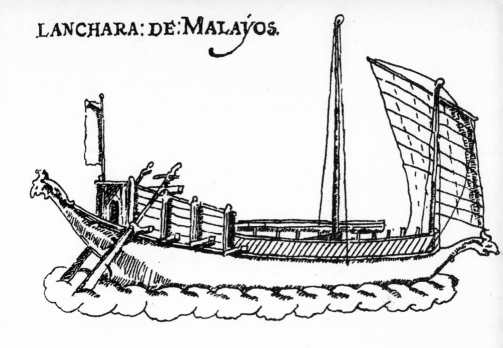

LANCHARA: DE: MALAYOS.

4 The long-standing juxtaposition of Malay and Chinese cultures in Malaya is reflected in this Portuguese early-seventeenth-century comparison of Malay and Chinese ship designs.

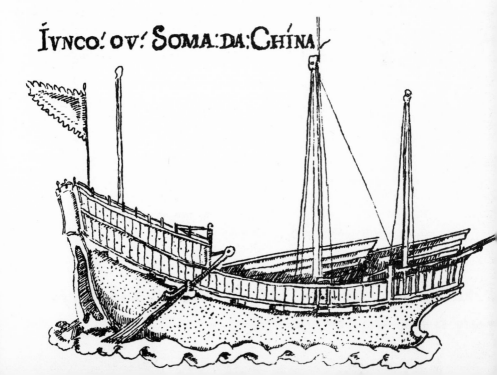

ÍVNCO: OV: SOMA: DA: CHÍNA

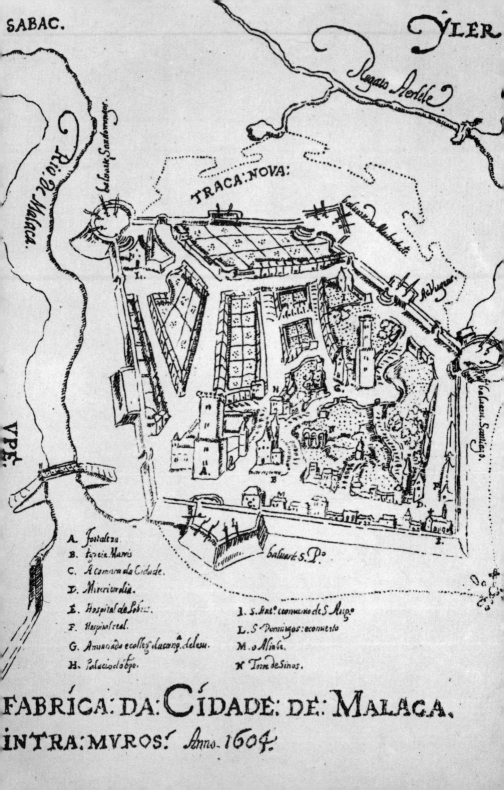

SABAC.

YLER

Regato Merlele.

Rio De Malaca.

baluarte Santo...

TRACA NOVA

VPÉ

baluarte S. Po.

A. Fortaleza
B. Igreia Matris
C. A camera da Cidade.
D. Misericordia
E. Hospital de Pobres.
F. Hospital real.
G. Anunciada e colleg da cõpª de Iesu.
H. Palacio do bpo.

I. S. Antº e conuento de S. Agº
L. S. Domingos e conuento
M. O Moinho
N. Torre de Sinos

FABRICA: DA: CIDADE: DE: MALACA.
INTRA: MVROS: Anno. 1604.

NCO: DE: ALBOQVERQV: 40:

RETRATO: DE: MICER: FRANCISCO: XAVIER
DA: ORDEM: DA: COMP. DE: IESV. Anno. 1542.

IHS

5 Malacca remained a key settlement throughout the Colonial period. This map of the City was made in 1604 (*far left*).

6 The Portuguese conquest of Malacca was led by Alphonso d'Albuquerque the second Governor-General of the Indies.

7 Portuguese coat of arms from a brass cannon.

8 As a result of missionary activity and the Portuguese policy of intermarriage, there were 7,400 Christians living in Malacca by 1613. St Francis Xavier was once buried in St Paul's Church there.

9 The Dutch did not capture Malacca until 1641, the Portuguese withstanding several attacks such as this one in 1606 by an alliance of Dutch with Malay soldiers of the Kingdom of Johore.

10 Malacca then became mainly a fortress town for the protection of Dutch trading interests.

11 The tombstone is one of many in St Paul's churchyard, Malacca, dating from this period.

12 This early-nineteenth-century engraving of a typically Dutch drawbridge at Malacca, with a pair of old cannon barrels on the river bank illustrates the Dutch power over a Malay-Chinese populace.

2   The People of Malaya

WHEREAS ENGLAND (50,331 square miles) contains a population of some 43 million, and (to take an American example) New
York (47,939 square miles) of some 17 million, the Federation of
Malaya, similar in area to England, had only 6,909,009 (mid-year
estimate 1960).[3] The distribution of this population was as under:

STATES	AREA IN SQUARE MILES	POPULATION MID-1960 (ESTIMATED)
Perak	7,980	1,344,411
Selangor	3,167	1,119,673
Negri Sembilan	2,565	407,809
Pahang	13,873	343,015
Johore	7,330	1,026,101
Malacca	640	323,348
Kedah	3,660	761,999
Perlis	310	98,761
Kelantan	5,750	553,001
Trengganu	5,027	306,942
Penang	398	623,949
	50,700	6,909,009

The break-down of the population into races was 3,460,956
Malaysians (comprising indigenous Malays and other Malaysians
from Indonesia), 2,552,276 Chinese, 772,880 Indians and Pakistanis, and 122,897 others.[4]

But in order to comprehend Malaya as a geographic, historical, and economic unity we must add to the above the figures for Singapore.

Singapore (as we must repeatedly insist) is very small in area, namely 224·5 square miles, about the same size as the Isle of Man or ten times the size of Manhattan, but it has a comparatively concentrated population, namely (December 1960 estimate) 1,665,400 – 1,253,400 Chinese, 232,400 Malaysians, 140,400 Indians and Pakistanis, and 13,700 others.[5]

On the face of things, therefore, Malaya's main problem is not one of overpopulation – that is if the economic circumstances are compared with those existing in (say) England or any other food importing country. But since the country is not yet selfsupporting in foodstuffs, the population it can support must depend upon the value of its exports to purchase the balance of foodstuffs and other commodities sufficient to maintain a reasonable standard of living.

The community statistics by themselves give the impression of three main racial groups existing on their own and (for all the reader can say) in different parts of the country. The actual facts are these. Although for the whole of the Federation the Malaysians out number the Chinese by some 900,000, in Penang, Perak, Selangor, Negri Sembilan, and Johore, the Chinese are in a majority; it is only in Malacca, Pahang, Kedah, Kelantan, Trengganu, and Perlis, that the Malaysians are the more numerous. The Chinese tend to be urban, but nearly everywhere, in town and village alike, the Malays (or Malaysians) live side by side with the Chinese and Indians, having daily contact with them for civic purposes as for trade – *but* without intermarrying with them, without sharing their religion or customs, and speaking different languages. Malay is the *lingua franca* for everyday purposes, as is English still for administra tion and the courts of law (though it is planned to replace it by Malay). Singapore on the other hand is 80 per cent Chinese.

Historically, Malaya is a 'Malay country', and this proposition is a main plank in the platforms of the Malay political parties, but how homogeneous the Malays are as a people we shall have to discuss in our later chapters. The practical fact is that whatever their country of origin, 'Malaysians' are nearly all Muslims, speak some variety of Malay, and fuse together readily into a single community. At the 1947 Census, when the 'Malaysians' were for the first time separately tabulated, out of a total of 2,544,000 for Malaya (includ' ing Singapore) there were 188,000 Javanese, 20,000 Boyanese, 11,000 Minangkabaus, 15,000 other Sumatra peoples, 62,000 Ban' jarese, and 7,000 Bugis.

This immigration of 'other Malaysians' into Malaya had been going on for centuries. Many of the indigenous Malays are of recent Indonesian origin (Negri Sembilan, for example, was colonized from Minangkabau, in Sumatra, in the eighteenth century). Never' theless, as we must insist, diversity of place of origin does not upset the social solidarity of the Malaysians *politically*. East Coast Malays may feel themselves quite different from West Coast Malays in some respects, but they are all bound together by the fact that (*a*) they are all Muslims, and (*b*) that even if they arrived in Malaya yesterday, they are all automatically 'subjects of the Rulers' of the States and, as such, Malayan citizens. At the same time it must be emphasized that this solidarity is only of recent growth and that at the time of the British intervention in the 1870s there was a sense of apartness among the various groups of Malays which made them regard one another as 'foreigners'. It was the increase in the number of Chinese which was the greatest force in binding the Malays into one community in self protection.

What distinguishes a 'Malay' or a 'Malaysian' from the other denizens of these parts? We shall see, when we come to our historical review, something of the diversity of Malay racial origins, yet the physical type as it exists today is sufficiently homogeneous to be quite distinctive. The complexion of the Malays has been described as being everything from olive'green to bronze or red, from brown to fawn, mahogany, or tea'rose. These descriptions may all be true of individuals and depend to a large extent on the degree of exposure to the sun. The quality that their skins have most in common is a liveliness and a mellowness that pleases. It is in contrast to the sallowness or oily blackness of some other races in the East. It gives off something; it glows with a light of its own. It is as wholesome as a new loaf. As for the eye, its colour ranges from black to deep brown. The Malay usually has a trim well-proportioned figure, but he tends to be shorter in the lower leg than Europeans. His nose is rather flat at the bridge (another mongoloid characteristic). His jaws are prominent, but his mouth is wide and good-humoured. He usually has a pleasant smile. Malays retain their boyish look and figure until well on in life.

The Malay's character has been variously described – sometimes in apparently contradictory terms. He is said to be both loyal and treacherous. We are told that his attachment to his sultan is one of unswerving devotion; that once a friend he is a friend for life. We are told that he is fickle and untrustworthy and that you never know where you have him. The fact is that, in their way, the opposites are probably true. He is loyal, but he is temperamental. He will serve you, but if you insult his dignity he may knife you – or at least *feel* like doing so. He is extremely proud. In an ordinary peasant you will find the punctilio of a Spanish hidalgo. But while his good manners are famous, he is subject to occasional brain-storms, when he sees red. This always arises from a real or imagined slight to his *amour propre*. If he broods long enough he may see the whole world as his enemy, and run amuck (the Malay word is *amok*, and the last syllable does not sound at all like 'muck', the k being a glottal stop), killing everyone in sight with his *parang*, the chopper with which he prunes his fruit trees and does a hundred other agricultural jobs. When he comes round he is rarely aware of what he has done. But to run amuck is quite an exceptional happening. (It was much commoner before British intervention because the Malay States had no asylums and homicidal maniacs were allowed to roam at large.)

The Malay has often been called 'lazy' – but anyone who has seen him toiling in the rice-fields, submerged sometimes nearly to the waist in water under a tropical sun, will realize that if the word 'lazy' can be applied to him it must have a special meaning in this context. The fact is that he does not see why he should spend his time sweating in a tin mine or in a factory when he can live on the produce of his coconuts or let out his few rubber trees to a Chinese contractor. The same sort of thing is true of his mental effort. In intelligence he is as good as any of his neighbours of other races, but it is difficult to stir him into the sort of mental effort that will, say, qualify him for one of the professions. The writer is once again tempted to blame the tropical sun for this dislike of exceptional effort, mental or physical, but he can hear the voice of the social anthropologist and the economist (off stage) sternly correcting him, insisting on social and political pressures or on the exigencies of 'subsistence agriculture' or capitalistic supply and demand. The fact remains that the immigrant races, especially the Chinese, are more industrious and enterprising than the Malaysians and this fact causes economic inequality between them and the native *ryat* (or *ra'ayat*, peasant) which has an important political bearing.

The above must suffice for an impression of the Malays and Malaysians, but before we pass on to the immigrant communities we must take at least a glance at a small group which have an even better claim than the Malays to be considered the original inhabitants of Malaya – namely the aboriginal tribes.

At the 1957 census, 41,360 persons of aboriginal stock were enumerated, as compared with 34,737 in 1947 and 31,382 in 1931. Of the total counted in 1947, 29,648 were nomads and the remaining 5,089 part of the general population. It would appear, however, that many settled aborigines returned themselves as 'Malays'.

The distribution of the aborigines was unequal through the States of the Federation, some 13,000 or so being in Negri Sambilan, 10,000 in Perak, and 5,000 in Kelantan, with a hundred or two each for the other States and Malacca and seventy or so in Penang.

Classification of the aboriginal tribes of Malaya and elsewhere has long been a matter of controversy among ethnologists, but an attempt at it was made by Mr H. D. Collings of the Singapore Museum in 1947. He divided them into three main groups: 1, Negrito; 2, Jakun; and 3, Semai, Sisek, Semelai, Temiar, etc., the Negritos totalling under 3,000 for the mainland, the Jakun something over 5,000, the Semai (Semak, Senoi) something over 7,000, and the Temiar (Temer, Temek, Tembel) approaching the same.

Collectively, all aborigines are known to the Malays as 'Sakais', ('subjects' or 'dependents'). They belong, however, to quite distinct racial stocks. The Negritos or *Semang*, are dark pygmy people with frizzy hair. They have intermarried freely with the other Sakais, who are an Indonesian people akin to the Dayaks of Borneo or the Bataks of Sumatra. Of those peoples the Negritos are the least advanced culturally. They are nomadic, living on jungle fruits and animals, and having no agriculture. Their weapons are bows and arrows and the blow-pipe. This last they are said to have borrowed from the light brown, wavy-haired Sakais. It shoots little poisoned darts. But whereas blow-pipes were common some thirty years ago, nowadays the Negritos rarely possess them. Whereas the Negritos live in mere palm-leaf shelters, the other 'Sakais' build pile houses, and plant millet, sugar, tobacco, plantains, and bill and rice. They move on after a harvest or two.

We now come to the second of the two main communities of Malaya, namely the Chinese.

Chinese immigration into Malaya belongs to historical times, and, as a leading phenomenon in the making of modern Malaya, we shall describe it in due place. What we give in this chapter is a brief account of their numbers, distribution, tribes, and functions in the Malaya of the 1960s.

The census for 1947 reveals how the Chinese community is divided into a number of tribes. The 'tribes' are linguistic divisions of groups speaking separate dialects, but nearly all the Chinese in Malaya originate in the Southeastern provinces of China, namely Kwangtung, Fukien, and Kwangsi (or Kwongsai). Taking Malaya as a whole (including Singapore) the numerical strength of the tribes in 1947 was (in round numbers) Hokkien (from the Amoy region of Fukien) 827,000, Cantonese (from Kwangtung) 642,000, Hakka (Kheh) (from the Kwangtung and Fukien borders) 437,000, Tiechius (Teochius) (from the Swatow region of Kwangtung) 364,000, Hainanese (Hailam) (from the island of Hainan) 158,000, Kwongsai 72,000, Hokchiu 48,000, Hokchia 13,000, Henghwa (Hinhoa) 17,000, and other tribes, 36,000.

The order of the tribes as regards numbers had remained un-altered since 1921.

Since the numbers of the tribes depended largely on immigration, and this was not constant for all tribes, their percentage increase has varied considerably – e.g. between 1931 and 1947 the Hokkiens increased by 53·6 per cent, the Cantonese by 53·7 per cent, and the Teochius by 74·6 per cent, but the Hakkas by only 37·4 per cent. The Hainanese also showed a high percentage increase (61·6) which was due not only to immigration but to the enormous improvement in the sex ratio which followed the raising of the customary ban in Hainan on the emigration of Hainanese women.

The mention of sex ratio calls attention to the disparity in the sexes, which caused a serious social problem before the Second World War. It led to a trade in women and girls for the purpose of prostitution which the Chinese Protectorate did its best to check. In 1931, there were only 620 Hokkien women (the Hokkiens are the oldest and most settled tribe) for every 1,000 males, as compared with 581 Cantonese, 526 Hakkas, 472 Teochius, and only 151 Hainanese. But with the practical cessation of immigration from China the sex ratio has tended to improve and the balance of the sexes has become much less of a social problem.

It is appropriate to insert a few words at this point on the changes which have come over Chinese society and the Chinese family in Malaya in recent years.

When they went abroad the Chinese took with them their own institutions. They brought, for example, ancestor worship and the clan and the family system. But with the coming of the 1911 Revolution in China and the influence of the West, which was particularly strong in the European colonies, these underwent great modification. Moreover, the experience of Chinese women had made them discontented with many features of the family system. Even thirty years ago, under Western influence, there had already been a change in attitude towards these institutions, but the whole-sale emancipation of women in Communist China carried the change to much greater lengths.

One sociologist (Maurice Freedman), writing of present-day

Singapore, concludes that while Chinese society takes its culture directly from Southeastern China, the economic and political conditions of the Colony are totally alien to the home setting and the social organization of the Chinese of Singapore cannot be understood simply as a branch of society in China. Chinese in the Colony, while preferring to seek their wives within their own dialect groups (and often within narrower divisions of these groups), treat the new marriage as a matter concerning only the bridal couple and their fellow household-members. In Singapore there has been a change in the relative status of primary and secondary wives (the 'principal wives' and 'concubines' of the older European literature on China) such that the latter have often assumed a significance probably unknown in China. At the same time, the definition of secondary wife has become much blurred, and there is a shading of polygamy into mistress-keeping. Divorce among Singapore Chinese is essentially a matter of mutual agreement between spouses. As for ancestor worship (says Freedman) what Chinese practise in Singapore nowadays is 'memorialism' rather than rites of ancestor worship or rites of kinship solidarity.

But let it not be thought that changes in family and marriage custom are confined to the Chinese of Malaya. The Malay and Indian women have also made great advances in recent years. A Malay man, being a Muslim, may have up to four wives at a time (if he can afford it!), but Malay women are more and more demanding that discarded wives must be adequately provided for. In any case, Malay women have always enjoyed far greater freedom than in other Muslim countries; there is no *purdah* system, women move about with perfect freedom with their faces only technically concealed by a shawl. They chat (and sometimes flirt) with the other sex in a way that their sisters in Egypt or Persia would not dare to do.

The distribution of the Chinese tribes in Malaya is partly due to historical accident. The Hokkiens, being the oldest community and largely engaged in trade, are the most numerous in the old Straits Settlements (Singapore, Penang, and Malacca); the Cantonese and Hakkas, who were originally mainly tin-miners, are in a majority in the Malay States as a whole. Apart from this, however, there does not appear to be any special significance in the fact that certain tribes are more numerous in certain areas – they tend to accumulate where their brethren are already settled. The Teochius are the most numerous in Kedah and the Hainanese in Trengganu, while the Hokchius continue to favour Singapore and the Kwongsis the districts of Lenggong. All Chinese engage in agricultural pursuits (though not much in rice-growing) – the Hakkas and Cantonese to the greatest relative extent, and the Hainanese and Hokchius to the least. The Hokkiens are of an urban habit because of their genius for trade and shop-keeping.

Having committed ourselves to an appraisal of the Malay character (however superficial) it would not be playing fair to refuse a similar temerity as regards the Chinese. Let us then attempt this appraisal. They are above all industrious and enterprising, willing to do work and take risks that few Europeans would do. They have a code of their own, a way of viewing the world quite different in inspiration from that of the European or the Malay. They are (in the writer's view) much more conditioned by *Tao*, the organic relationships of reality as they see it, than by Confucianism or Taoism or even by the fashionable ideologies of today. Modern political alignments have made no difference to the 'persona' the Chinese present to the world. They are still 'poker-faced' and non-committal; they still contrive to give the appearance of submission to authority (even while they are working against it). The visitor to Malaya who knew them in pre-Second World War days when they were so often the 'middlemen' between the British and the other communities would not notice any outward change. We have seen that their social and family system is undergoing a profound transformation and we shall see that they are being subjected to most powerful political pressures, but they are still the same people and their function is much the same as it was before Malaya became independent. Were it not for the Chinese and the British between them there would be no modern Malaya, for the Malays would not have been disposed to depart on their own from their traditional way of life.

The Chinese of Malaya (as we shall understand better when we come to discuss politics) are pulled in two ways – first by their

47

allegiances to China and Chinese ways, and second by their bonds with the land they live in. The former pull is likely to be stronger among the 'China-born' (nearly two-thirds of the total) but with the great reduction of immigration the Chinese community is becoming more settled and is bound to become more and more 'Malayan' in outlook. But more important even than political sympathies is education. The Chinese are virtually divided into the 'Chinese-educated' and the 'English-educated' – the former being more numerous, but the latter more influential in government since, although Malay is the 'official' language both of the Federation and Singapore, English continues to be the administrative language and the governing institutions of Malaya were shaped or created during the British régime. The great internal problem of the Chinese was to bridge the gap between these two cultural divisions (a leading objective of the 'English-educated' Prime Minister of Singapore, Lee Kuan-Yew); their wider problem was how to merge with the Malays, Indians, etc. in a common loyalty to Malaya. Superadded to this were the questions raised by the merger of the Federation, Singapore, and the Borneo territories into 'Malaysia'.

Intermarriage does not take place between the Malays and the non-Muslim communities of Malaya. A barrier is raised by the laws of Islam, but in practical terms boils down to simple taboos such as those against 'pork' and 'dogs'. Whereas in the Buddhist countries (Thailand, Burma, Vietnam, Cambodia, Laos) there is no barrier to intermarriage and the Chinese immigrants are, generally speak-ing, absorbed into the local community within three generations, Malaya is a different case. This is not to say that admixture has not taken place in the past between Chinese and Southern Asians (the Chinese of Old Malacca often married their Balinese slaves); it is merely that current prejudice made it rare.

Nevertheless, one must not convey an impression of a draconian segregation of the races. There is a borderland fringe – the occasional Chinese convert to Islam who describes himself in the census returns as 'Melayu' (Malay); the Chinese girl adopted in infancy by a Tamil and brought up as such; and the few cases in which the basic attractions of sex ignore the prohibitions of law and custom.

Apart from the distinction of nationality which has arisen between Indians and Pakistanis since 1947, local nomenclature has made it very difficult for the census enumerator to distinguish between those who originate from the two States of the sub-continent. To the ordinary people Southern Indians are all 'Klings' – a term derived from the ancient kingdom of Kalinga, but of which the Southern Indians themselves disapprove; every other Indian is a 'Bengali' to Malays and Chinese, irrespective of geographical or racial origins. But of the 900,000 or so Indians and Pakistanis in Malaya, some nine-tenths are from South India (Tamils, Telegus, Malayali, etc.); the remaining tenth are from North India and Pakistan (Sikhs, Punjabis, Pathans, Bengalis, Gujerati, etc., etc.). Nearly half of the South Indians are to be found in Perak and Selangor alone – two States for which the Punjabis and Sikhs also show a predilection.

Between 1931 and 1947 the number of Indians (including those who later became Pakistanis) declined by 6·3 per cent, owing to the ravages of the Japanese occupation, but has since risen again. The great majority are employed as labourers on the rubber estates, but Indians and Pakistanis are also active in commerce, and there are a number in the professions of law and medicine. Their relatively small number has limited their importance in politics and business, but the Malayan Indian Congress has since independence constituted a section of the Alliance Party, and there have been several ministers of Indian or Pakistani origin.

The Europeans in 1947 totalled 31,000; the Eurasians 9,000. The 'other races' (of great variety, from Sinhalese to Siamese and Persians to Jews) totalled 17,000 for the Federation. In 1957 the numbers had not appreciably changed.

Architecturally speaking, it must be remembered that Malaya has had a very short history. The Malay houses at the time of British intervention were very simple in design, and had not even the pretensions of the Batak dwellings of Sumatra with their pinnacled roofs of thatch. In Malacca, the Portuguese period is marked by the ruins of St Paul's Church where St Francis Xavier was once buried, and the old gate of the fort, and the Dutch are remembered by their brick-red Stadthuys (1641–60) and church and some quaint wrought-iron weather-vanes. Penang, too, with over a century and a half of building history, and helped by the veneer of tropical lichens, gives off a hint of respectable age. Yet it is the Chinese temples in the towns and in the limestone caves of Perak, with their winged roofs whose porcelain figurines are silhouetted against the sky and their bulbous yellow lanterns painted with vermilion characters, which best convey a sense of oriental mystery and exotic charm. In Penang there are a hundred of them, ranging from the great Buddhist temple of the 'Great Extremes' at Ayer Itam to the Goddess of Mercy Temple in Pitt Street, filled with gilded images and clouds of incense. Little wayside shrines are dedicated to the local deity, Ta Peh Kong.

But, generally speaking, it is solidity and utility that we must expect from Malayan buildings rather than architectural beauty. Kuala Lumpur, the capital of the Federation, boasts a gigantic rail-way station with Islamic towers and minarets and a big domed mosque – legacies of the first great rubber boom of 1910. Since independence, building has gone ahead at a great pace and through-out Malaya and Singapore huge blocks of buildings loom up where yesterday there was nothing to be seen, and all are of that 'packing-case' type which you will find everywhere in the 1960s from Istanbul to Paris, and from Detroit to Tokyo. It is the age of the 'functional', and this is quite in keeping with the spirit inherited from the British Raj under which Order, Health, and Cleanliness were the presiding deities and those brazen hussies, Taste and Elegance, were *not* invited to Government House.

The smaller towns of Malaya follow a standard pattern with minor peculiarities. There is first a grid of streets at right angles to one another, fronted by a row of Chinese shop-houses. The 'shop-house' always has a colonnade, at street level. (In Malaya there are no 'pavements' or 'side-walks', there are only 'five-foot ways'.) At a distance away there is the inevitable *padang* (a large rectangular grass lawn of startling green) which is lined by the government buildings, the post office, and the mosque. The hospital is usually about a quarter of a mile or so from the town.

The houses in the residential areas all have gardens. Those gardens take a deal of tending, for the jungle is always on the look-out to recover its own. Buildings abandoned only for a few years are swallowed in trees and creepers, and it is no uncommon thing to see a tree sprouting from the roof of a house.

Yet, when all is said and done, the 'real Malaya' is still to be found in the *kampongs* which look much the same as they did before the British came. Here the houses are raised from the ground; the roofs are of thatch (*atap*); the walls are of thatch or of wood. Round the house there are, as there have always been, the fruit trees (mangosteen, rambutans, bananas, papayas), groundnuts, vegetables, coconuts, and sometimes rubber. The only 'British period' innovation in the kampongs is drainage and the supply of pure water laid on through hydrants. How to bring to the Malay *rayat* the same standard of living as is enjoyed by the other communities is (as we shall see) an outstanding problem in Malaya – but at least he has already enough to eat.

In Malaya there are no ruins comparable to those of Borobodur or Prambanan in Java, but these were the achievements of a people closely related to the Malays and indications of a similar talent to theirs are apparent in Malay arts and crafts. These have suffered from the impact of industrialism with its mass-produced imports. During the British period a stimulus to keep them alive was provided by the Malayan Arts and Crafts Society. With independence, the Government has striven further to encourage their revival.

But support to the current belief that early Malayan architecture was indigenous or Indonesian in inspiration, and not the product of Indian colonization, is given by Dr Lamb's recent excavations of an eighth–ninth-century temple in Kedah.[6]

The nearness of India made Indian cloths and Indian patterns the favourites of the court in the days of the Malacca Kingdom. The Malay word for silk is borrowed from the Sanskrit and silks were first introduced from India. At the present day, silk-weaving is practised only in the coastal states, especially in Kelantan, Patani and Trengganu, and some of the larger towns elsewhere. That it has survived on the East Coast may not be unconnected with the fact that the Empire of Sri Vijaya included this area of the Peninsula. One striking type of cloth still manufactured in Trengganu for sarongs and other garments is one in which, as in the Indian fashion, a pattern of gold thread is interwoven with the silk, sometimes with plain silk, sometimes with silk chequered with thin lines in white or blue (*Kain tenggarun*), sometimes with silk of mottled 'line' pattern. Patani, Pahang, and Selangor produce cotton cloths with a small pattern on a dark green or dark blue ground which is polished with cowrie shells, stamped with carved wooden blocks that have been smeared with gum and then covered with gold leaf that adheres to the gummy pattern. Yet another process is to impress a pattern on silk by means of small stamps containing only a single flower or section of a border.

'Fine mats' are recorded by Chinese chroniclers as exports from Johore three centuries ago, and today Malay mat- and basket-makers yield to none in skill and artistry. There are three chief methods of adornment – in mats, open-work and the interweaving of strips dyed red, black, and yellow to produce diaper patterns; in mats and especially in baskets, the plaiting of raised fancy twists by a method practised in Malacca and termed the 'mad plait'.

Silverwork is another craft in which Malays have excelled. There are still two predominant styles, a northern and a southern, both pre-Islamic and indebted to India for their designs. In both styles waist-buckles of silver, gold, and niello are ornamented with the large Buddhist lotus-blossom. Some caskets have deep gadroons forming lotus petals like those at the base of Buddhist idols. In Perak open lotus-blooms like tiny roses abound on watch-shaped caskets and decorative bands on large lidded bowls. The more expert the Malay smith, the more the flowers and foliage tend towards the naturalistic – the peony and the chrysanthemum being their favourite motifs.

As common as *repoussé* is a kind of filigree for neck pendants, brooches, *keris*-sheaths, etc.

Much artistic skill was expended by Malay craftsmen in the ornamentation of the traditional Malay weapon, the *keris* (or creese as Milton and Tennyson called it). Keris hilts commonly represent

Vishnu's bird, the Garuda (wingless but sometimes beaked). There is also the Raksasa hilt which stands for the demon cannibal Kalmasapada. Kerises are still manufactured, though now only as 'curios' – not for use.

Modern Malay pottery follows traditional patterns. The herring-bone pattern is characteristic of modern pottery from Perlis. In Perak, water vessels in the form of a gourd reproduce bronze-age flasks; common in Malacca are spouted water-jars of a kind used many centuries ago. But the Malay potter has long lost his inventiveness and artistry in this machine age.

But more even than in their crafts, the traditional Malay artistry survives in the two elaborate rituals of Hindu origin which are still enacted. One is the enthronement ceremony of a Malay sultan, and the other is the ceremony that is performed as a preliminary to dramatic performances. The 'shadow-play' is repeated at harvests, weddings, or circumcision festivals. The episodes are from the Ramayana. Wearing the yellow scarf appropriate to gods and kings about his shoulders, the reciter of the play in Kelantan claims to be the reincarnation of Vishnu. Cross-legged he sits before a tray of offerings for the spirits of the four quarters of the worlds, spirits of ocean and forest, Ganesha, Arjuna, Sang Bima, and the Bhutas. There is a special plate of uncooked rice, and there are a raw egg, raw thread, and money for Siva, as supreme teacher, and for him in his form of Nataraja, lord of dancers and king of actors. Then wafting the incense from his censer, the reciter begs the leather puppets that represent Siva and Vishnu to drive away all spirits of evil.[7]

Like the Malays, the Chinese of Malaya, too, have inherited something of their ancestral crafts and culture. Their clothing now is mass-produced and standardized, as are their kitchen utensils, but you will still occasionally see a Chinese nonya (matron) wearing her old-style flowered dress with gold bodkins sticking out of her coiffure cemented with rice-paste, and the old-style wedding has not yet completely disappeared (though one hears of, rather than sees the rare example). Chinese crafts, however, survive mainly in the repro-duction of images for the Buddhist temples or in figurines sur-mounting their winged roofs. So it is with the Indians and Pakistanis.

In the case of the southern Indians (Tamils, Malayalams, etc.) they have inherited the gods of the Hindu pantheon direct without any intervention and replacement from Islam, and their temples in many towns of Malaya have the same intricacy and variety in their terraced façades as have those of their Indian homeland, and at the great festival of *Thaipusam* they bring out the silver car of Siva, which is preceded in the procession by devotees, some with skewers piercing both cheeks and tongue as a gesture of atonement.

The cultural renaissance which has been in progress in China in recent decades has also extended to the Malayan Chinese and inspired them to write poetry and to paint. The poetry is mostly of the *vers libre* description, and the painting is usually in the traditional style – though often with happy results. Malaya has also produced one or two novelists since the war, notably Chin Kee⁄Onn, the author of *Ma⁄ri⁄ee*. Cultural societies are numerous among all the communities.

The late Loke Wan⁄Tho was known internationally as an ornithologist and as a photographer of birds. Han Suyin, the author of *A Many⁄Splendoured Thing*, lives in Johore Bahru.

It is the modern world which first impinges on the attention of the visitor to Malaya, but the ancient world is still active among its peoples. How far are those latent forces comingling and influencing one another? It is perhaps in the 'amusement parks', the great fair⁄grounds of Singapore, Kuala Lumpur, and Penang, that an answer is suggested to the question. Here you will find in progress a Chinese play featuring characters from the Han dynasty, not far away an orchestra playing Indian music such as the last King of Golconda may have listened to, and at another short distance a *wayang* will be in progress – a peculiarly Malay dramatic form with lively burlesque (often including 'Hamlet' with characters in top⁄hats!). Not all of the audience is of the race for which this entertainment is primarily intended, and the stray Chinese, Malays, or Indians halting for a while to enjoy a new experience may well be functioning as un⁄conscious transmitters of culture within this 'plural society'.

Inter⁄communal cultural activities are sponsored by societies such as the China Society of Singapore. At one typical 'rice⁄dumpling' party held by the President of the Society to celebrate the Dragon Boat Festival there was a recital of Chinese poems translated into English, Malay and Tamil, followed by a performance of Indian dancing.

But quite apart from any 'osmosis' on the artistic level, for a truly 'Malayan' outlook to evolve there must be also a modification of the separate racial social institutions through intercourse. To some considerable and largely unacknowledged extent this has already taken place. The 'Baba' Chinese of Malacca or Penang who has forgotten his ancestral tongue and speaks only a kind of Malay or English is already 'Malayanized'; even Europeans who reside for long in the country become unconsciously 'Malayanized' (as their compatriots detect when they come home). As legislation proceeds it is bound to be influenced by the institutions of one community or the other. There is nothing basically incompatible between them, nor for that matter have all Malays identical customs (while those of other parts of Malaya are 'patriarchal', those of Negri Sembilan are 'matrilineal' if not fully 'matriarchal'). Remember, too, that the customs of all the communities are subject to the same modern influences and pressures. Malay, Chinese, and Indian women have alike been to the forefront claiming emancipation from their traditional bonds. As regards complete racial fusion, this cannot be achieved so long as the Muslim taboos remain, but miscegenation between Indian and Malay has taken place on a considerable scale in Penang (not always between Muslims) and great changes can be wrought in social attitudes within a generation or so.

13 Many of the aboriginal tribes in Malaya remain nomadic, living on jungle fruits and animals and using bows and arrows and blow-pipes as weapons. This was how Sir Hugh Low, the most able and humanitarian of early British administrators in Malaya, found them in the 1880s.

14 The more advanced aboriginals build villages like this, which is in the Cameron Highlands, one of Malaya's beauty spots.

15 Rice, first introduced into Malaya from India a thousand years ago, remains the staple food.

16 The typical Malay settlement, or *kampong*, has changed little during the centuries.

17 The Malay peasant and the Chinese trader is symbolic of a long-standing relationship between the two races.

18 Trade attracts Chinese of all classes and all ages.

19 Malay settlement is traditionally riverine, water providing the best possible means of transport through the jungle in the absence of roads and railways.

20 Most of the 900,0[..] Indians and Pakistanis [...] Malaya are employed [...] labourers on rubber estate[...]

21 A great majority [...] them come from Sou[...] India. They constitute t[...] smallest of the three ma[...] racial groups in Malaya b[...] their culture remains qu[...] distinct from that of t[...] Chinese or the Malay[...] These Tamils are perform[...] ing the Hindu ritual Dan[...] of Devils.

22 Malay kite-flying is still practised in the coastal States of Trengganu and Kelantan where competitions are held at festivals.

23 In the villages, the Ota Ota, a traditional Malay dance with sword and shield, continues to be performed.

24-25 The manufacture of Batik cloth and basket work are two of the Malay crafts encouraged by the present government.

26 Temples reflect much of the best of Chinese craftsmanship. This is one of a hundred in Penang.

27 A performance of Chinese opera on a stage in one of the amusement parks in Singapore is attended by both Chinese and Malays.

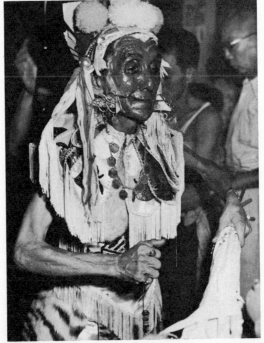

28 Chinese funeral procession in Kuala Lumpur.

29 Chinese religious beliefs are multiple and eclectic. But ancestor worship and the belief in spirits is basic to them. A spirit medium here incarnates the Monkey God.

30 Traditional Mala[y]
ture is seen at its best i[n the]
elaboration of cerem[onial]
at enthronements and [wed-]
dings. This is the Sul[tan of]
Kedah and his bri[de in]
wedding costume.

31 The formal in[stalla-]
tion of the Undan[g of]
Jelebu, one of the [chiefs]
of Negri Sembilan. [The]
ceremony was post[poned]
for twelve years unt[il the]
Central Governmen[t of]
newly independent M[alaya]
voted £500 to enable [it to]
take place.

3   The Age of Imperialism

THE IMAGE OF 'IMPERIALISM' imposed on the world by Communism is one of callous aggression and ruthless greed. Certainly the progress of Western ambition in Asia had a very seamy side, and no attempt will be made here to cover up its crimes. The forcible 'opening' of China, beginning with the Opium War was without doubt a sorry episode and one of which present-day Westerners, and Britons in particular, should for the most part be ashamed. But even in this episode the spirit was 'mercantile', not 'conquering'. There was nothing of '*la Gloire*', of the spirit of Napoleon and his *Grande Armée*, or of Alexander and his mission of intermarrying humanity by force. In British colonial expansion into Malaya there was none of the ruthless glorying in conquest of a Tamburlaine

> Threatening the world with high astounding terms
> And scourging Kingdoms with his conquering sword

but a will to make the world safe for trade, even though the *actual* intervention, when it came in 1874, was inspired by the fear that if Britain did not intervene in the Malay States to create order, some rival Power *would*.

The extension of British authority in India was an expensive business, and it worried the hard-headed directors of the East India Company. The territorial acquisitions of Wellesley, Ellenborough, and Dalhousie were due to the forward policy of the man-on-the-spot, moved either by ambition or strategic necessity; the occupation of the Dutch colonies during the French wars was also strategic: it was only when some practical need decreed it that the directors and, for the most part, the Governors-General, would acquiesce in the establishment of a new post. Such was the case with the founding both of Penang and Singapore.

In the course of the wars with the French or during the north-east monsoon which roared across the Bay of Bengal from October to April, British ships had to send round to Bombay to refit, there being no natural harbours on the Coromandel coast. The directors there-fore sought a 'careening station', a port where their ships could be provisioned or repaired. They also sought a place wherein to grow spices to compete with the Dutch monopoly. What appeared to be suitable for both purposes was found for them in the island of Penang (108 square miles) which, through the agency of Captain Francis Light, was ceded to the British in 1786 in perpetuity in return for an annual rent of 6,000 Spanish dollars. In 1800, a strip on the mainland named Province Wellesley was added to the Settle-ment and the combined rent was increased to 10,000 Spanish dollars.

Alas, Penang (or Prince of Wales Island) proved unsuitable as a 'careening station' (the wood not being suitable for shipbuilding or repairing). The pepper, nutmegs, and cloves, moreover, after a period of successful cultivation, ceased to be really profitable.

The story of Thomas Stamford Raffles and the firm establishment of the British in the Straits of Malacca has often been told, but we must tell it shortly once again.

In spite of the unpromising start made by Penang, the directors (misled by the over-optimistic reports of their servants) conceived the most grandiose expectations for its future, and in 1805 promoted it to be the Fourth Presidency of India, on an equality with Bengal, Madras, and Bombay. One of the minor appointments to the Government staff was Raffles, a promising clerk at the Company's head office but without 'background' and largely self-educated, as an Assistant Secretary. He learnt Malay on the five-months journey out to Penang.

Raffles's great chance came when in 1811 he was appointed Lieutenant-Governor of the newly subdued colony of Java, the centre of the Dutch East Indian possessions. He ruled over these territories for five years and left them not very long before they were handed back to the Dutch under the Treaty of Vienna. On his return to the East after his leave in England (he met Napoleon in St Helena in 1817 on the way home and wrote him off as an arrogant boor) the only job the directors could offer him was the LieutenantGovernorship of the white elephant settlement of Bencoolen. From Bencoolen Raffles looked abroad and decided that one reason for Penang's failure as a naval station was that the Straits were too wide at that point for effective patrolling by sailing ships; where the settlement ought to have been, he said, was at the narrow entrance to the Straits to the south, which, moreover, was at the conflux of a network of trade routes.

In 1818, Raffles visited Calcutta and was able to induce the GovernorGeneral, Lord Hastings, to authorize him to sail with a small expedition in search of the new station he had in mind. Hastings soon changed his mind, but by the time that his counterinstructions reached Raffles, the latter had progressed so far in his negotiations as to justify a 'reference back' to Calcutta with a consequent saving delay.

The place that Raffles had fixed upon for his new station was the island of Singapore, off the southern tip of the Peninsula. It was then in the possession of the Temenggong of Johore with a population of about eighty Malays ('Orang Laut' or 'ProtoMalays') and forty Chinese. In return for protection and 3,000 Spanish dollars a year, the Temenggong signed an agreement for the cession of the island to the East India Company. Further to secure the legal possession of the island, Raffles then negotiated with Tunku Long, then resident on the Dutch island of Rhio (Riau), whom Raffles, with the Temonggong's endorsement, recognized as the legitimate Sultan of Johore. The sultan was to receive an annual pension of 5,000 Spanish dollars (in addition to the Temenggong's 3,000 dollars).

Neither Penang nor Singapore, it will be seen, was 'conquered' by the British. So far, so good. But the one great problem was that Singapore was within what the Dutch claimed as their sphere of action. Directly they heard of these proceedings they were bound to raise a hullabaloo. And raise a hullabaloo they did!

There then ensued a bitter 'paper war', but since it took about ten months for letters to be exchanged between Singapore and London there were considerable intervals between the shots. It seemed at one time as if the British Foreign Secretary was on the point of capitulating to Dutch demands (Holland was traditionally important in British foreign policy as the custodian of the River Scheldt). But while an invaluable delay was caused by the official and diplomatic interchanges, Raffles's new settlement was proving itself a success. Under a free-trade policy, immigrants flocked in, including a considerable number of Chinese. In the cold light of a century and a half later, comparison of Raffles's population figures with those more impartially established, reveals that the former exceed the latter by about three to one and it is probable that enthusiasm made him see treble. The decisive fact was that Canning at the Foreign Office now felt that Singapore offered too much promise of success lightly to be surrendered to the Dutch, and this coloured his negotiations with them.

In March 1824 a treaty was signed between Britain and Holland settling their outstanding differences in Asia. Holland ceded to Britain all the Dutch 'factories' (stations) in India and 'Malacca' (the Dutch name for the entire Malay Peninsula) and withdrew all objections to the British occupation of Singapore. In return, Britain ceded Bencoolen to the Dutch. The Dutch undertook to make no further treaties with the rulers in the Malay Peninsula, while the British gave a similar pledge both with regard to Sumatra and to the islands south of Singapore. There were also a number of other commercial and political provisions.

Britain had now three dependencies in the Malay Peninsula – Singapore, Penang, and Malacca. Only Singapore, of the three, was paying its way. In 1830, Penang was reduced to the status of a Residency from a Presidency. Singapore became the capital, and the Straits Settlements, as they were now called, were to be directly subordinate to India.

The Anglo-Dutch Treaty of 1824 left the Malay Peninsula with two 'Powers' overshadowing it – Britain and Siam. The spheres of influence of neither Power was precisely delimited, however. The

Siamese regarded the Malay states which lay close to their southern borders as vassals. In order to extend their influence farther south in the Peninsula, the King of Siam, in 1816, ordered the Sultan of Kedah to invade Perak and to insist that that state should send to Bangkok the *Bunga Mas*, or 'golden flower', the symbol of a vassal's submission to his feudal lord. This was pure aggression, since Perak was independent of Siam. It was clear when the Straits Settlements were established that unless the British were to see the whole of the mainland pass under the Siamese they would have to come to an understanding with them as regards the extent of their respective spheres.

The external history of the Malay states in the first three-quarters of the nineteenth century was governed by treaty relationships. The Burney Treaty of 1826 between Britain and Siam provided that the Siamese were to remain in control of Kedah, and that while Siam undertook not to 'go and molest, attack or disturb' Perak and Selangor, the British also undertook to leave Perak alone and to ensure that Selangor did not attack Perak. The position of Kelantan and Trengganu was left vague by the wording of the treaty.

The Straits Settlements were now prospering in spite of the piracy which was endemic in Malayan waters and which menaced shipping at the very entrance to the harbours. Nevertheless the Settlements did not pay their way, and up to the end of the East India Company in 1858 were always a burden on it. The Straits Settlements, wishing to be freed from Indian control, had first to prove to the home government that they could pay their own way, and having eventually succeeded in doing so, they were transferred from the India office to the Colonial Office in 1867.

In the meantime, the Malay states of the Peninsula were in a condition of political decay approaching anarchy. There was constant warfare between the sultans, and civil war between chiefs or rival claimants to a throne was almost as frequent. The authority of the sultans had decayed, so that there was nothing to check the feuds of the petty rajas. One authority has likened the conditions on the mainland to that of England in the reign of Stephen. Trouble between the Malays and the Chinese miners working the tin-mines in Larut was an added complication after the middle of the century when new deposits of tin ore were discovered there. Moreover, the Chinese were divided by adherence to one or other of two rival Secret Societies, the Ghee Hin and the Hai San (both branches of the Triad). A Secret Society would commonly signalize a success in a fight with a rival society by dyeing its members' shirts in the blood of the vanquished. They fought on sea as well as on land and made the trade along the Perak coast impossible.

Pressure on the British to reverse their attitude of 'non-intervention' came from the Chinese merchants of the Straits Settlements who were financially interested in the trade with the interior. They petitioned the Government, together with the British merchants, on many occasions to intervene to restore, or create, order. But for long the home government refused to listen to these petitions. The answer given was that if merchants chose to take risks in pursuit of profit, that was their affair. The Malay culture was a very old one. The incantations of its magicians may well be an echo from ancient Babylon; from Hinduism it derived its notions of kingship (even of 'the divine right of kings to govern wrong'), and Islam had implanted fatalism into the Malay character over some five hundred years. But theocracy elsewhere had long been in decline and Malay society, shot through with abuses and anachronisms, was overdue for a change.

In order to justify the intervention of Britain in the Malay states, which took place from 1874 onwards, it would be a fair procedure to show that the régime which the British introduced was superior to and brought more happiness to the people than the one it replaced – though this alone would not, by modern standards, excuse aggression in the first place. But in giving a true impression of Malay society in the 1870s, any suggestion of British self-righteousness or essential superiority must be avoided. The Western reader must never be allowed to forget that revolutions in a state of society are happenings usually over short spaces of time. In England as recently as 1810, Lords Eldon, Ellenborough, and others, had declared that if the law which made it possible to hang a child for stealing five shillings were repealed, no one would be able to sleep safely in their beds; that in the eighteenth century and beyond lunatics were chained up and treated with gross barbarity; and as to the abuses still existing well past the middle of the nineteenth century (imprisonment for debt, child labour, flogging, semi-starvation through unemployment) we have only to look to the novels of Dickens, Charles Reade, Hardy, and others. So if the Malay reader is satisfied that a *historical* and not a *moral* attitude is being adopted in describing the Malay states of the 1870s he will be less likely to dispute the accuracy of the picture here presented.

Malaya was mostly jungle and swamp and was very sparsely peopled. In 1850 there may have been about 300,000 persons in the Malay states in an area where there are seven million today. Settlement was confined to strips along the coast and the main rivers. Each state was self-sufficient, and there was no idea of a 'Malay World' or of a union of Malay states. The old dominant states of Malacca and Johore (the Malay 'empires' of the past) had long since disappeared. A Malay hailing from another state was regarded as a 'foreigner'. The 'Malays' themselves were often of recent 'foreign' origin – from Minangkabau, Korinchi, Rawa, Acheh, Java; small groups of Arab–Malay descent, Bugis, etc. Islam was the main binding force, together with the common culture of the Malays.

All foreign observers of Malay society at this period agree that a great gulf existed between the aristocracy and the *rayats*, or common people. The latter existed only to serve and obey the former and to minister to their comfort. The sultan was the source of all authority, and he alone (theoretically at least) had powers of life and death. But the chiefs, in point of fact, had a great measure of independent control over their districts, due as much to isolation as any other factor, and they had a say in determining the succession to the throne. The revenue of the district was the personal income of the chief who had, however, an obligation to remit a proportion of it to the sultan. Each chief maintained his own private army.

By the system of *kerah* (*corvée*), the chief could call for compulsory labour for all purposes and for any length of time, decided solely by his wishes. There was no payment for this forced labour though the village headmen would normally provide food for the workers.

Slavery was another institution which bore heavily on the common people. The *Malay Annals* relate how the Bendahara of the last Sultan of Malacca had so many slaves that if one of them arrived at his kampong smartly dressed he would be mistaken for a stranger and invited up to the house, until his identity was discovered and he was ordered to sit with the other slaves and menials. Even today the descendants of slaves are looked down upon. When the British started to administer Perak they found not only debt-bondsmen but four kinds of slaves proper, namely (1) captives taken in war; (2) pagans like the Sakai who were hunted down and captured; (3) manslayers and other criminals who were unable to pay 'blood money', and who surrendered themselves *and their families* to the Raja as slaves; and (4) the children of a female slave other than those acknowledged as his by her owner. To these had to be added Abyssinian and negro slaves brought back from Mecca by wealthy pilgrims. The total number of slaves and debt-bondsmen in Perak about 1874 was estimated at about an eighth to a tenth of the then population; 'the ownership of a number of slaves and debt-bondsmen was a mark of a man of rank, wealth and influence'. If a slave girl was married, her husband had to accompany her into bondage. The tortures inflicted on royal slaves at the period of British intervention in Pahang in 1888 have been described in all their horror by Sir Hugh Clifford. Criminals (as in Siam) were often chained together and herded into dark and noisome dungeons.

Most oppressive of all was the system of debt-slavery, a system alien to Islamic law, but occurring in various forms among the Hindus. If a man could not pay a debt he became the slave of his creditor until the debt was discharged. Redemption in Perak could theoretically be purchased for 25 dollars (100 *bidor*), but actually this payment was often refused and much bigger sums were demanded. Sometimes fictitious debts were invented to secure a person as a slave and he was forthwith dragged from his home into servitude. No work that a debt-slave performed for his master was set off against the debt. Sometimes the master fed and clothed debt-slaves; more often they had to supply themselves with all necessities.

Again, in spite of the rule that the wife and children of a debtor should not be liable for his debt, unless it were incurred with their knowledge, and that a widow of a debt-slave should not be liable for more than one-third of her husband's debt, creditors would often hold the wife and family of a debtor in bondage for the full amount during his lifetime and after his death. The daughters of a debt-bondsman were given in marriage by the creditor who took the dower or held the bridegroom in bondage until he could pay it. No part of the dower went towards the extinction of the girl's family debt. 'The monstrous injustice (says Sir William Maxwell) was of modern introduction or there would be few but debt-bondsmen among the population.' As in Siam, Burma, and Ceylon, even the free cultivator was not free from feudal service to his overlords as one of the conditions of tenancy.

But whatever the injustices imposed on the ordinary Malays, it cannot be pretended that the British had any right to invade native sovereignty to reform them. Nor is it true for that matter that intervention, when it came, was prompted by any motive of reform – at least on the part of the British home Government – though once intervention had taken place it was inevitable that these abuses should awaken the British conscience. Nor was the British Government persuaded to act primarily with the object of improving the conditions of trade. It seems clear from recent research that the actual change of policy to permit intervention which took place when Mr Gladstone's first Government was still in power and Lord Kimberley was Secretary of State for the Colonies was inspired by a fear that if Britain took no action another European Power would establish a station in the Straits.

In 1873, the newly appointed Governor of the Straits Settlements, Sir Andrew Clarke, received instructions from the Colonial Office to use British influence 'with a view to rescuing, if possible, those fertile and productive countries [the Malay States] from the ruin which would befall them if the present disorders continue unchecked'. Sir Andrew decided to interpret these instructions in an active sense – and even, if necessary, to exceed them.

The opportunity for intervention was provided by the situation in Perak. In this state there was a disputed succession to the throne and a civil war between the Chinese Secret Societies. Ismail had been installed as sultan by the chiefs in departure from the traditional line of succession and overlooking both the claims of the Raja Muda, Abdullah, and the even more 'legitimate' claim of Yusof. Clarke decided to recognize Abdullah (the Raja Muda or 'heir apparent' under the previous reign) as the legitimate Sultan.

It should be stressed that the succession to the throne in a Malay state was usually decided by established custom, but was nevertheless elective. Thus, in Perak, the order of precedence was the Sultan, the Raja Muda (or heir apparent), and the Raja Bendahara. On the death of a sultan the Raja Muda moved up one to fill the space at the top, and another princeling, usually the eldest son of the dead ruler, became in turn Bendahara. All the ranks were elective, but trouble came only when the presumptive heir was (as in the case of Yusof) unpopular with the chiefs.[8]

Clarke first of all sent an officer (W. A. Pickering, the first Protector of Chinese) to meet the rival Chinese leaders in Penang to discover whether they were prepared to reach an agreement and accept the arbitration of the Governor of the Straits Settlements. When Pickering reported a favourable outcome to his talks, Clarke proceeded to invite the leading chiefs to meet him at the island of Pangkor near the estuary of the Perak River in mid-January 1874. None of the Perak chiefs, except the Mantri, attended the meeting; Ismail was invited, but did not come, while Yusof was not even invited. Abdullah was recognized as Sultan, and signed an agreement to accept a British Resident *whose advice must be asked and acted upon on all questions other than those touching Malay religion and custom.* This wording was to be the basis of the British protectorate system which lasted (with the interruption of the Japanese occupation) until the Federation became independent in 1957.

Soon after this (March 1874) Selangor accepted a Resident on similar terms, and by the end of the year there was likewise a British Assistant Resident stationed in Sungei Ujong, the principal of the nine states which later were joined to form Negri Sembilan.

The question from the beginning was how 'advice' was to make an effective method of indirect rule. Since most matters of government were regulated by 'Malay religion and custom', this left the Residents very little to advise upon. If British supervision was to be made effective it had to be by reason of the persuasiveness of the Residents.

If this were so, J. W. W. Birch, the first British Resident in Perak, certainly went to work in a fashion that was calculated to fail. Birch was a typical product of Victorian evangelical self-righteousness. His attitude towards Abdullah, the sultan recognized by the Pangkor Engagement, was that of a schoolmaster towards a delinquent schoolboy. Birch was determined to abolish debt-slavery and to collect the revenues for the use of the State. Since the British Government was not prepared at this stage to bring pressure on Abdullah to declare debt-slavery illegal, Birch resorted to indirect measures (such as giving shelter to refugee female bondsmen in his Residency). As regards the revenues, he proceeded to collect them direct, thus depriving the chiefs of their incomes before he had arranged to give them paid employment or to pension them off. Moreover, on Birch's advice, the Governor of the Straits Settlements had decided to govern the state directly through 'Queens' Commissioners' in the name of the sultan. The consequence was that the Malay chiefs met in secret conclave and resolved that Birch should be murdered. And murdered he was, on 2 November 1875, as he was engaged in posting proclamations declaring the powers of the 'Queens' Commissioners' at villages along the banks of the Perak River.

The Governor of the Straits Settlements, Sir William Jervois, anticipating that Birch's murder would be followed by a general Malay rising, telegraphed the Colonial Office for large reinforcements from India and Hong Kong. These arrived, but turned out to be unnecessary since the Malays had no concerted plans and the opposition to the British collapsed after some limited resistance. By the end of the year fighting had ceased, and by mid-1876 all the leaders had been rounded up. The Maharaja Lela (who had actually ordered Birch's murder) and a few others were tried and executed. Abdullah and two other chiefs were banished to the Seychelles.

Order having been restored, the British Government had to decide what policy they would adopt and they were resolutely opposed to annexation. In the event they decided to give the Resident system another trial. This time, applied by a series of able British officers over a period of years, it was made to work and the sultans were persuaded to 'ask for and act on British advice' consistently so that the whole face of Malaya rapidly became transformed, the country was developed, and it eventually emerged as a modern state.

British protection was extended to what became known as Negri Sembilan (the nine states) in stages. Sungei Ujong, the most important of the nine states, had already accepted a Resident, and in 1886 Jelebu, and 1887 Rembau also accepted British protection; in 1889 the rest of the small states followed suit, and finally the federal state of Negri Sembilan came into being in 1898 under a leading prince (Yang di-Pertuan Besar) with a single British Resident. All this was accomplished peacefully and with the willing consent of the chiefs. In the case of Pahang, however, some pressure was used. This state had long been in disorder, and in February 1888 the stabbing of a Chinese British subject, Go Hin, outside the palace on the sultan's orders, brought stern reproof from the Governor of the Straits Settlements, and in August the sultan made his submission to Queen Victoria and asked for a British Resident.

Outstanding among the Residents was Sir Hugh Low, Resident of Perak from 1877–89. Low, aged over fifty when he took up his appointment, had started life as a botanist and had spent most of the previous thirty years of his career in Borneo. He spoke fluent Malay and judiciously blended great tact and patience with an occasional show of firmness. The principal instrument used by him in making 'advice' work was the State Council, an institution first brought into existence by himself. This was presided over by the sultan and the other members included the leading Malay chiefs, Chinese leaders, and the Resident himself. In working through the State Council, Low fully utilized the British system of compromise – if a measure was opposed it was modified; if it was extremely unpopular it was dropped. Only in extremely rare cases was the Council over-ridden. This principle was the one on which British administration in Malaya was henceforth exercised. It was one by which European expertise was made to operate with the willing co-operation of the Malay sultans, chiefs, and the non-Malay communities. The same principle applied when the Federal Council was created in 1909. It continued in force until the Federation of Malaya became independent in 1957.

'Happy is the country without a history', and it has been remarked that Malayan history after 1875 was 'mainly statistical'. That is to say that order having been created, there were no more wars to record, and no violence or 'exciting' murders on any scale. Thus, to bring our summary of the British period down to its virtual termina-tion with Malayan independence, we have only to mention certain outstanding constitutional events and then to outline the great administrative, economic, and social development which took place under British protection.

The chief events were the Federation of the states of Perak, Selangor, Negri Sembilan, and Pahang in 1896, the Treaty of Bangkok of 1909, whereby Siam transferred its sovereignty over the four northern Malay states (Kedah, Perlis, Kelantan, and Treng-ganu) to Britain, and the Decentralization policy of 1935. The latter was intended to restore to the separate Federated States some-thing of the autonomy they had lost through federation. It should also be mentioned that in the case of Johore, which for long had been a virtual dependency of Singapore, its relations with Britain were at length specifically defined in a treaty of 1914.[9]

4   The British Record

ON ASSUMING THEIR somewhat nebulous 'advisory' function, the early Residents had to feel their way cautiously and while they were doing so they had to build up an administration to implement the policy for which they were able to gain acceptance from the Rulers. Only a few (including Swettenham) were trained administrators – one was a colourful adventurer, another an ex-coffee planter, another a Singapore lawyer, and Low, the greatest of them all, was, as we have seen, a botanist. But in the conditions of the time they served their purpose well and in a situation in which one professional administrator, Birch, had failed. Sir Frank Swettenham, himself a professional civil servant, remarked long after his retirement that while the locally recruited types 'filled the bill' at the time, it became necessary to have university trained officials, appointed by competitive examination, plus selection, when the administration and the legislation became more developed and complex.

The early problem, apart from defining 'advice', was financial. Low was faced with all the difficulties of revenue collection which had confronted Birch and with a heavy war debt in addition. He had to create a police force to replace the troops, and to do it cheaply. He reduced the cost of the police by conferring police duties on local headmen. The question of revenue collection he solved by making the chiefs the local headmen and allowing them a substantial percentage of all Government dues collected in their districts. Before appointing the headmen he consulted the opinion of the people of the district. The feudal right of the State to *corvée*, or labour-conscription, he replaced by a land-tax, and made a profit for the

State in doing it. The consequence was that Perak was completely free from debt by 1883.

We have heard already of Low's creation of a 'State Council'. Whether or not the idea was originated by Sir William Jervois or Lord Carnarvon is subsidiary to the fact that it was Low who first put the idea into practice. The sultan was President of the Council, which combined the functions of the Executive and Legislative Councils in the Straits Settlements. Although the sultan was President, he could only come to a decision with the approval of the other members, and the Resident could often get his way by (tact fully) carrying the Council with him in opposition to the sultan. But once decisions were taken they became Orders in Council with the full force of law. The Council appropriated to itself the regula tion of all important matters, many of which had hitherto fallen under the jurisdiction of local chiefs, it dealt with the budget, appointed Malay chiefs and headmen and fixed their salaries, and confirmed or modified death sentences passed in the Courts. The experiment was so successful that it was copied by the other states under British protection.

Low, as British Resident, could not ignore the debt slavery which had caused Birch such trouble, but he was careful to adopt different methods in dealing with it. The development of a money economy in place of a system of feudal obligations meant that it tended to be more advantageous to pay wages than to keep slaves. Also the fact that the State now undertook responsibility for defence and order meant that personal armed retainers were neither required nor allowed. Then on 1 January 1884, slavery and bondage came to an end by law and compensation was paid to the former masters.

But in spite of these reforms, the Malay states were still far from having a modern state of society. If there was to be any considerable improvement as regards health, education, welfare, and housing, money in large quantities was required. This could be obtained only through economic development. And for economic development to take place, communications had to be vastly improved, and an adequate labour supply had to be ensured.

In short, Malaya had to be conducted through the processes which

Britain had passed during the Industrial Revolution from 1760–1840. In Malaya these processes had been set in train by changes in world economic conditions long before British intervention. The establishment of order and the institution of the Resident system made it possible to accelerate the revolution. The obvious fields for development and increased revenue lay in mining and agriculture.

Henceforth the history of Malaya is written largely in the annual reports of the Residents and the Governors of the Straits Settlements. Then, as administration became more complex, these were amplified by the annual departmental reports.

Malaya is not particularly rich in mineral resources, except for tin. Gold exists in small quantities in alluvial deposits, and was recovered with great labour by Malays and Chinese, but the only lode mine of importance was that at Raub in Pahang, exploited from 1889 by Australian capital but since almost worked out. Malaya has no anthracite coal, only lignite, and though the Batu Arang mines extracted large quantities after the formation of Malayan collieries in 1913, the deposits have since become exhausted and the industry is dying. Iron-ore was later on mined by Japanese enterprise in Johore, Trengganu, and Kelantan since shortly after the First World War, and by 1938 the shipments represented about half of Japan's iron supply. The mining of bauxite (aluminium) belongs to the twentieth century. About ninety per cent of Malayan mining today is of tin, and at the time of British intervention in the Malay states the proportion was even higher.

But European enterprise in the tin industry was a late post-intervention development and it was the Chinese who held something like a monopoly of the industry for many years to come. We have already seen how the discovery of new deposits in Kinta caused an influx of Chinese miners from the middle of the nineteenth century onwards with consequences of historical significance. It was they who introduced the more advanced 'open-cast' (*lombong*) method of mining in place of the Malay *lampan* method, which consisted in diverting a stream to wash away the earth from the tin-ore.

The Chinese, too, were quick to adopt Western devices, and about 1879 when Hugh Low imported a British steam-engine and centrifugal pump for flood prevention and put them on show, the Chinese miners at once placed orders for them.

It was not, however, until the late 1880s and early 1890s that tin-mining attracted European capital. About this time there was an increased demand for tin-plate in the West especially for canning food, etc., and this stimulated European interest in the industry. And with European capital came even more efficient mining methods such as improved hydraulic machinery and eventually, in the next century, the tin-dredge, whose capital cost was so considerable that it was beyond the resources of all but Western-capitalized concerns. The consequence was that whereas the Chinese up to 1912 owned nearly 80 per cent of the tin-mines and Europeans only 20 per cent, by the fourth decade or so of the twentieth century the proportions were practically reversed. By 1904, Malaya was producing about 50,000 tons a year and the Malayan revenues were greatly increased by the export dues.

The shortcoming of tin-mining, however, is that, unlike agriculture, it is a wasting asset and once the metal is taken out of the ground nature does not replace it. Early in the 1930s a committee of British experts reported that Malayan tin deposits would be exhausted in about forty years. In consequence the Government established a tin-revenue replacement fund, which, however, was diverted to war purposes during the Second World War. In 1962, considerable new tin deposits were discovered in Perak.

The export duty on tin was always heavy. In Larut in 1874-5 it was 25 per cent or more of the value of the tin and this probably is representative of the traditional dues. In more recent years it has fluctuated between 10 and 15 per cent of the value, and nowadays an income tax of 30 per cent on the net profits of the mining companies has made tin-mining a much less profitable enterprise. Nevertheless, large fortunes have been made, and are still being made, from tin.

In 1930 the net amount of capital invested in tin dredging was £13,099,431, the total area allocated for tin-mining in 1938 was

184,237 acres. In 1930 the price of tin was £144 a ton; during the Korean war (1950–1) £1,600 a ton; it was about £858 in 1961. In that year 56,000 tons were produced.

Although the economists disagree violently on many matters, they seem to share the opinion that 'subsistence agriculture' represents a very primitive stage in human evolution and that transition to 'cash crops' marked an advance. Certainly, if the Malays had been left to themselves, they would have remained communally self-sufficient, maintaining a nice balance between the amount of food needed and growable and the number of hands available to grow it. All the Malayan agricultural products grown for sale today were introduced from abroad. Apart from spices, nothing grown by the indigenous people was commercially valuable, and even rice, which had become the staple food, was introduced by Indians in the first millennium of the Christian era into a country better fitted by nature to the cultivation of yams.

Pepper had been grown for export in the seventeenth century; spices were grown in Penang after the British obtained it, and they were also grown in early Singapore. Chinese agriculturalists introduced pepper growing into Johore after 1840. In the 1830s a few European merchants planted sugar-cane in Penang, Province Wellesley and Malacca. Sugar proved to be the crop *par excellence* for the Chinese cultivator who devoted infinite care to the preparation of the ground. In 1846 the Imperial Government decided to admit the sugar and rum of Province Wellesley, etc. into the home market at the reduced colonial market rate whilst the products of Singapore (because it was an entrepôt for imported sugar from China, Java, and Manila and it would have been difficult to distinguish between locally grown and imported sugar) were charged foreign duties. This was a death-blow to Singapore sugar-planting and at the same time the duties charged on Singapore sugar gave a great impetus to sugar-planting in Penang and Malacca. European speculators were not slow to take advantage of the situation, but improved on the primitive Chinese methods of extracting and refining the product. Sugar had its day in the Malay states as well, but after indentured labour was abolished in the Federated Malay States in 1910, the Malayan sugar industry declined, and the last factory closed in 1913. But for about 50 years sugar had been the most important agricultural product.

Coffee had also enjoyed a short innings. In the 1880s coffee planters arrived from Ceylon where their crops had failed owing to an outbreak of a plant disease. They planted Liberian coffee in Perak, Selangor, and Negri Sembilan and for a time they did well. Then, at the end of the century, coffee prices dropped sharply owing to an increased output of Arabian coffee in Brazil, and a few years later the Malayan crops were seriously damaged by pests. The planters either went back to England or turned to the new crop – rubber, which was destined to exceed the earlier crops by far in profit-making.

After Low, Henry Ridley, appointed Director of Gardens, Singapore, in 1888, was probably the man who did most to make rubber-growing practicable and to promote the growing of it. (It is pleasant to record that he lived to be over 100, dying in the late 1950s.) Owing to his researches and exertions a few private growers started small plantations, but by 1897 only 345 acres were under rubber. By 1906, however, the commodity for the first time became profitable, and by 1910 the rubber boom was at its height. In that year the price was 12s (U.S. $3) a pound; in 1932 it was $2\frac{1}{2}d$ a pound; in 1961, 2s 2d. The annual production in the early 1960s was over 600,000 tons.

To control the wide fluctuation in the price of rubber, in the 1920s the rubber-growing interests persuaded the British Government to authorize a scheme for the restriction of output (the Stevenson scheme), which failed owing to the refusal of the Dutch East Indies to join in. A new agreement, however, to restrict exports on a quota basis was signed between the British, Dutch, French, and Siamese governments in 1934.

The rubber was grown not only by big estates but by smallholders (of less than 100 acres). By 1937 under this scheme, Malaya had 3,302,170 acres under rubber, 2,026,348 being estates of over 100 acres (both European and Asian owned) and 1,275,822 acres

83

being Asian smallholdings. The net export of rubber in 1937 was 681,638 tons.

A Rubber Research Institute was founded in Kuala Lumpur in 1926 to carry on the work hitherto undertaken by the Department of Agriculture and the Rubber Growers' Association – including experiments in budding and grafting from selected trees, selective weeding, treatment of soils, and the search for new uses for rubber. In 1947 over one-fifth of the men and one-third of the women 'gainfully employed' in Malaya were employed in the cultivation of rubber.

Among the other crops grown, the coconut came first, and a large proportion of the nuts (in about 1930, 50 nuts per annum per head of the 4 million population) were for home consumption. The oil-palm was introduced from West Africa during the British period, reaching Singapore via Ceylon and Kew in 1875. Pineapple cultivation for earning was begun by Europeans in Singapore Island in 1880, but it was not until the 1920s and 1930s that it became a big industry through Chinese enterprise. The cocoa-tree, although introduced long ago, was still only in its experimental stage commercially at the time of the Japanese invasion.

To enable agriculture, mining, and commerce to take place it was obviously necessary that there should be an adequate system of communications. At the moment of British intervention, there were no roads, and communication was confined to the Straits, the China Sea, the rivers, and a few jungle paths. (Those who have read any of the accounts of jungle warfare in the 1948–58 period will be able to form some notion of the isolation of the settled clearings from one another in those pioneer days.)

Railways received first priority and roads were first designed to serve the railway rather than to compete with it or duplicate it. The early lines were fairly short, connecting the tin producing areas with the west coast – Taiping to Port Weld (1885), Kuala Lumpur to Bukit Kuda (1886), then to Klang (1890) and later to Port Swettenham (1899), Seremban to Port Dickson (1891), Tapah Road to Telok Anson (1893). After the Federation of 1896, a north–south line joined up the existing railroads and continued northwards to Prai (opposite Penang) and southwards to the Johore border at Gemas. It was not until 1909 that the line was extended to Johore Bahru in the south, and then the extension to the north into Kedah was joined up with the Siamese railway in 1918. It was then that a start was made with the east coast railway joining Gemas and Siam, which, owing to financial and constructional difficulties, was not opened until 1931. Even then the east coast line had a restricted value. The Japanese removed its rails during their occupation for use in Siam, and it was not restored until 1948.

Like the railways, the roads had to be constructed as funds became available from the revenues. They generally followed a north–south course and it was only later that a road across Pahang from west to east was drawn through the jungle. Much of this region was un-populated, and the great trees, the 'lords of the forest', with no branches for the first sixty feet or so, reared themselves up in silence for many miles along the fine road to connect the scattered kampongs. Road construction in Malaya (especially of roads up to the hill stations) called for considerable engineering skill, and Malayan roads became famous for their quality. Although today there are only about 6,500 miles of roads in Malaya (A1=43 miles, A2=1,828 miles in 1960) the system compares favourably with those of the other countries of Southeast Asia.

A modern system of communications, however, was primarily of benefit to industry and commerce, though this in time brought greatly increased revenues. How were those revenues spent, and how did this expenditure benefit the quickly growing population?

The way in which the British tackled the health problem in Malaya deserves a chapter to itself, but we are restricted here to an outline. The establishment of Town Sanitary Boards was an important initial step. Not only did they supervise the lighting of streets and the upkeep of roads and houses, but they looked after the clearing of the streets, built drains, and provided piped-water.

Medical research was set to work simultaneously to investigate the causes of the worst diseases. Vaccination was introduced (though in the face of some local opposition); cholera was checked by improved hygiene. In 1900 an Institute of Medical Research was established. One of the first diseases it tackled was beri-beri, and the theory that it was due to diet deficiency was now established. The consequence was that with supplementary diets the death rate from the disease was quickly reduced.

But it was in respect to malaria that the anti-disease campaign obtained its most spectacular results. In 1897 (Sir) Robert Ross had traced malaria to the female of the anopheles mosquito, and this vital knowledge was first approved in Malaya by (Sir) Malcolm Watson (by a happy coincidence a nephew of Ross). Arriving in Klang in 1901, he found the area in the throes of a malaria epidemic; the hospitals were full and hundreds were dying. Obtaining a grant from the Government, Watson drained the area systematically and destroyed most of the breeding-grounds of the anopheles. Within a year he had reduced the death rate from 168 to 41 per thousand and had in doing so saved Port Swettenham, recently built at great cost, from being abandoned.

This system was then extended to other areas in Malaya. But the drainage, the removal of undergrowth, and the oiling of streams was extremely costly, and had it not been for the revenues from rubber and tin it would have been impracticable. During their occupation, the Japanese discontinued these measures (relying on prophylactics for their own troops) with the result that malaria of the malignant variety reappeared and renewed its ravages.

It remains to be noted that the Singapore Medical School, founded in 1905, in 1910 became the King Edward VII College of Medicine, and was, with Raffles College, established after the First World War, amalgamated to form the nucleus of the University of Malaya after the Second World War.

Colonial régimes have been accused of starving their colonial peoples of the means to knowledge – education. How far was this accusation justified as regards Malaya?

To begin with, it was left to missionary bodies or individuals to start schools. The Penang Free School (1816) was a notable example;

Raffles's Singapore Institution (1823) was another, but the latter was planned more as an institute for the comparative study of Oriental and Western cultures and was over-ambitious for the period. The many schools that were started later on were of more modest aim. The mission or trustee-type schools were in due course given grants by the Straits Settlements and FMS (Federated Malay States) Governments.

But Government-run schools, in which the medium of instruction was either English or Malay had been established from the 1890s onwards, and by 1919 in Malaya there were 17 Government English Schools as against 63 schools of a trustee or mission type, aided, but not controlled by the Government. Then, in 1905 a Malay College was established at Kuala Kangsar, which was a boarding school for the sons of princely families, intended primarily for the training of candidates for careers in the Malayan Civil Service.

To provide vocational training for the many was mooted, but a commission appointed in 1918 was against the proposal since it was considered that Asians still preferred clerical to manual employ-ment (the traditional belief that it is ungentlemanly to work with one's hands remained strong). But later on trade schools were opened, and the changed conditions due to the slumps in tin and rubber meant that technical training became more popular, clerkships being more and more difficult to obtain. The first trade-school was started in the FMS for Malays, and Malay was the medium of instruction, but since employers demanded a knowledge of English a class in that language was added. Fitters, motor mechanics, and tailors were turned out by the schools. Schools for teaching carpentry were started later. The success of those schools, together with the slump of 1930-2 which caused clerical unemployment, led to trade schools for all races being started in the Straits Settlements and Federated Malay States.

In the Malay states the teaching of Malay was concentrated upon, and instruction was also given in handicrafts and physical training. The curriculum of the girls' schools included domestic science, needlework and clay modelling. In the Malay schools there were no fees, and attendance was compulsory for all Malay boys between the ages of seven and fourteen who lived within one and a half miles of a school. For Malay girls primary education was also free, but not compulsory. The Sultan Idris College at Tanjong Malim trained Malay teachers for the whole of Malaya, and a Translation Bureau attached to the College translated text-books into Malay.

The provision of Tamil schools by estates was compulsory where there were ten or more Tamil children.

From an early time the Chinese in Malaya had provided their own schools. In Kuala Lumpur, by way of an exception, the Government built the first Chinese school, but the *Capitan China*, Yap Ah Loy, provided a schoolmaster at his own expense and other leading towkays (Chinese heads of businesses) supported the school. Up to the First World War and after, there were not many schools relative to total population and the majority of them were still 'Old Style' – that is to say, they taught reading and writing and the Confucian classics, the *Four Books* (*The Great Learning*, *The Doctrine of the Mean*, the *Analects*, and *Mencius*) which were learnt by rote. But the drive for modern education in China, which had been given a great impetus by the Revolution of 1911, had for some time been increasingly felt in Malaya. In 1917, Dr Hu Shih had started the National Language Movement in China to make education more accessible to the masses by replacing the literary language with all its difficulties and complexities by *Kuo Yü*, or 'mandarin', as the medium of instruction. This movement caught on in Malaya in the 1920s and within a few years all the Chinese schools were of the modern type and all used *Kuo Yü*.

In the early years, the Chinese schools were established and maintained by the Chinese themselves without Government assistance, but from the 1920s onwards they increasingly accepted Government grants-in-aid and these grants became such an important part of the schools' finances that they could not carry on without them. There was no interference by the Government with the curriculum, though the advice and assistance of the Staff of the Education Department were made use of by the schools, but political doctrines of a subversive nature were not permitted. The text-books all came from China, were impregnated with the spirit of Chinese Nationalism, and made no mention of the existence of Malaya.

When, in a moment, we take account of Chinese immigration into Malaya, we shall understand better the political problems involved, but it should be explained here that the 'subversion' in question was mostly of the Chinese Nationalist kind, namely the propagation of the doctrine that 'Wherever there are Chinese, there is China'. As we shall see, the Chinese community in Malaya was subjected to pulls both from China and elsewhere, and the controversy over the question whether education was to be in Chinese, Malay or English was one of the leading features in post-independence Malayan politics.

After the British had established their protectorate system, the population of Malaya increased by leaps and bounds. In 1911 it was about 2·3 million, in 1931 3·8 million, in 1947 4·9 million, and in 1957 6·3 million. Between the 1850s and the 1950s the population of Malaya must have increased (and here inadequate early estimates make guesswork necessary) by something like eighteen times. This was partly due to natural increase, greatly favoured by the improvement in health and sanitation and the consequent prospect of a longer life, and partly by immigration.

The immigrants were of several racial types. The 'Malaysians' from Indonesia were nearly all Muslims and they merged readily into the Malay community. In 1931 the number of 'All Malaysians' to 'Malays Proper' was (for all Malaya including Singapore) 1·9 million to 1·6 million; in 1947 it was 2·4 million to 2·1 million. The Indian community had increased from 445,000 in 1921 to 582,000 in 1931, but had fallen to 545,000 in 1947. But the most numerous immigrants were from China. The Chinese community grew from 1·17 million in 1921 to 1·7 million in 1931, 2·6 million in 1947, and 3·8 million in 1960.

Immigration was not controlled until the unemployment caused by the world depression of 1929-32. The bulk of the Indians came in from South India to work on the rubber plantations; the Chinese came in to work on the tin-mines and also to follow the hundred and one different trades and occupations which arise under a 'money economy'. They were not only labourers but traders and artisans, tending to be urban rather than rural, though about half a million of them 'squatted' in the country districts during the Japanese occupation to grow food. These squatters became a problem during the Communist rising of 1948–60 when many of them assisted the Communist guerillas in the jungle with manpower and supplies and were consequently resettled in the 'new villages' where a closer control could be exercised over their activities. There was practically no business activity, wholesale or retail, in which the Chinese did not engage, and Helmut G. Callis estimated that in 1937 the total Chinese investments in Malaya approximated to U.S. $200 million (approximately £40 million) as compared with the other foreign investments amounting to U.S. $454·5 million (approximately £90·9 million).

Immigration on this scale, however, turned Malaya into a 'plural society', that is to say one in which the different racial communities lived side by side without intermarrying and with different standards of living.

Finally, a word or two must be said about labour and labour legislation in the British period.

The Malayan Labour Code was the product of many years of experience, and had been amended a dozen times or more, the particular object of its solicitude being the Tamil labourer. It contained provisions regarding wages, housing, sanitation, labour agreements, and general conditions in places of employment. The 'truck' system whereby an employer made a labourer take part of his wages in kind, or had to buy from his employer, was forbidden. After the abolition of indentured labour in 1910, Indian labour was largely recruited through *kanganies*, or recruiting agents. But with the increasing attractiveness of conditions in Malaya, there was a great increase in the numbers of Indian labourers who found their way to the country on their own. By 1937, 88·8 per cent were recruited.

Among the provisions of the Code in the interests of the Indian labourer were those requiring that maternity allowance must be paid to female labourers, and that they should be given two months leave after the birth of a child; all hospital expenses of a labourer and his dependents had to be paid by the employer; a crèche with food and attendants had to be provided for children under three; children under ten were not to be employed, and estate schools had to be maintained free. A minimum wage was laid down according to 'zones', and in fixing it account was taken of the following elements – enough rice and other foodstuffs for a reasonable diet, clothing, festival expenses, and a trip to India every three years, maintenance of dependents, and monthly saving of about $1.

An agent of the Government of India was appointed to Malaya in 1923, and his duty was to safeguard the interests of the Indian labourer, in co-operation with the Labour Department.

The Chinese labourer was not legislated for in such a thorough-going way. The assumption was that he was well able to look after himself, and in spite of the fact that no minimum, or standard, wage was fixed for him, he invariably received a higher rate of pay than a Tamil. But he suffered from the 'contract' system, and the many ingenious devices of contractors or employers to 'squeeze' him, and he more and more became the subject of special legislation. It was not easy to enforce these provisions, for the Chinese labourer had a strong preference for piece-work.

Factories and workshops were regulated by law, most of its provisions being on the Western model.

Labour organization by the labourers themselves was still in an embryo state at the time of the Japanese invasion. Among Chinese the traditional practice had been for the employer and employed to belong to the same guild; but later the tendency had been for separate associations to be formed, and in 1940 the Government passed legislation to facilitate the formation of trade unions. To help the men to learn how to manage their own unions, they were allowed to have persons outside their particular industry on the union committees.

The charge made both by Communists and Socialists is that Malaya was 'exploited'. By this is meant that the only motive for developing it was the profit of investors.

No doubt foreign capital did draw out a large profit from Malaya over the years. In doing so, however, it provided Malaya with industries that are her main sources of revenue now that she is independent. If profits are still exported, it is only after the imposition of the maximum tax which the independent Malayan Government calculates that the rubber, tin, and other industries will bear. It can be demonstrated that the financial interests in Leadenhall Street, Mincing Lane, and Wall Street (it must be remembered that there was also considerable United States, French, Belgian, and other foreign capital invested in Malayan rubber), having no direct contact with Malaya, were interested exclusively in profits. But their agents on the spot were in contact with the Malayan people and in dealing with them applied in general the standards of enlightened humanity. The Colonial Governors, either directly in the case of the Straits Settlements, or working through the Treaties of Protection in the case of the Malay states, had obligations primarily to the people of the country and their legislative and executive powers were subject to a great degree of control by the Legislative, Federal, and State Councils. They were, it is true, appointed by the Colonial Secretary, who was a politician. These Secretaries of State were usually representative of 'City' interests, and those who visited Malaya at intervals during the inter-war years were interested primarily in the rubber and tin industries, not in the people of whom they knew next to nothing. The Colonial Office itself was remote from Malaya (very few of its officials ever came anywhere near Malaya), but it did act as a restraining influence on the politicians and the 'City'.

Wages were low and no doubt they should in many cases have been higher. But they were regulated mainly by supply and demand and the cost of living, and they had to be high enough to attract immigrant labour. They were in fact higher than elsewhere in Asia except Japan. An effective trade-union movement was the one great lack in British Malaya, but the Governments could not create it on their own initiative and they did (somewhat belatedly perhaps) encourage its growth.

When a country supports a population between fifteen and twenty times as large as it was a century earlier, it is obvious that it must have become vastly richer in order to do so. But it is argued that the Malay *rayat* or peasant remained largely outside this 'money economy', and that his standard of living was not improved by Malaya's wealth. It is true that the Malay peasant possessed very small purchasing power (as low as M $2–4 a month perhaps for a majority), and the problem of raising this standard to the level of that enjoyed by the other communities is a fundamental aim in post-independence politics, but the *rayat*'s standard of living cannot be gauged purely in terms of money. The *rayat* is a rice-producer and under the British the best rice-land was reserved for Malays (1913). During the Japanese occupation he was much better off than, for example, the urban Chinese, for he at least had enough to eat. He also had his fruit-trees, tapioca, etc. and often a little rubber (which, however, he usually preferred to let out to Chinese to tap). He has no rent to pay. (Winstedt mentions that some years ago when it was proposed to employ in London a Malay of this rustic background it was calculated that £600 a year would scarcely suffice to procure him amenities equal to those to which he was used.)

A commentary on the relative wealth of the Malay peasant and the rural non-Malays was provided in January 1962, when Mr Chin See-Yin, the independent member for Seremban, said in the Malayan House of Representatives, 'It is not true that the non-Malays are necessarily richer than the Malays. In the kampongs Malays own farming land, but in the new (Chinese) villages the people own nothing. Therefore they are land hungry.'

Another charge was that the British system of government in Malaya was 'undemocratic', that there was no representation of the people. It is certainly true that there were no elected legislatures, but the Straits Settlements had elected municipal commissioners quite early on. The legislatures were designed to give representation to the various communities and interests. For example, the Federal Legislative Council in 1939 had 15 official members and 12 unofficial representing the minority communities, industry, trade, etc., and the legislature of the 1948 Federation had 50 seats for unofficial members representing labour, planting (public companies and smallholders equally), mining, commerce, agriculture, professional, educational, and cultural representatives, and representatives of the Chinese, Indian, Ceylonese, and Eurasian communities. To say that the British opposed or hindered the growth of democratic institutions is untrue. There was no popular demand before the Second World War for popular representation, and the British could scarcely be expected to generate this demand. The fact that the urge to democracy was so slow in developing was due primarily to the 'plural' nature of Malayan society and the suspicions of the main communities, Malay and Chinese, of one another. Each looked to the British to protect them against the other. Thus was 'paternalism' perpetuated.

What the British cannot escape, however, is responsibility for the mass immigration that turned Malaya into a 'plural' society. Yet without the immigrants Malaya would not now be a highly developed country. It has been well said that modern Malaya is the joint product of British and Chinese enterprise. It was the task of the independent governments to see that the Malays shared more equally in the riches that have thus accrued.

One advantage that arose from the 'paternalistic' nature of Malayan society under the British was that the Malayan Civil Service (MCS) could do its work without political pressures. Malaya was outstandingly well administered, and to the efficiency and fairness of the Malayan Civil Service, Tunku Abdul Rahman, the post-independence Prime Minister of the Federation of Malaya, has paid tribute on more than one occasion.[10]

What is likely to prove to be the point most open to criticism when Britain's case comes before the tribunal of history is the British policy towards the Malayan Chinese. Even if their families had been in Malaya for hundreds of years they were still treated as aliens. They were barred from the Malayan Civil Service, they were not 'subjects of the Rulers', and except in the Straits Settlements (where the locally born were British subjects) the most they could aspire to was to be granted passports as 'British protected persons' (a status, however, that was legally dubious). They were also discriminated against in many other ways. Although their immigration into Malaya in large numbers was permitted and even encouraged by the British,

94

no attempt was made to integrate them into the Malayan community. Only about 10 per cent of the Malayan Civil Service had any knowledge of the Chinese language. Thus it was that the Chinese had to make their own terms with the Malays, their status in the negotiations being that of 'second-class citizens'.

Nevertheless, it must be conceded that the British were right in assuming a responsibility to protect the Malays from the more commercially-minded immigrants. Before racial equality could be fully conceded, there must be a period of transition during which the indigenous people could learn to compete with the immigrants under modern conditions of free enterprise, and even after independence, many Malay leaders feel that this transitional period must be further prolonged.

32 From being an obscure clerk in the office of the East India Company, Stamford Raffles rose to acquire Singapore for the British and to be the main architect of its development in the early nineteenth century.

33 In 1832 Singapore became the capital of the British dependencies in the Straits of Malacca, nine years before this engraving of Government Hill was made.

34 Battles between Chinese secret societies menaced trade. This painting of the 1850s shows a peaceful demonstration of a secret society in Malacca.

35　The murder of J. W. W. Birch in 1875 while he was mediating between warring
secret societies, provided the opportunity for British intervention. Shown here are
British troops ascending the Perak river. This was the beginning of the Protectorate
system that lasted until 1957.

36 A British resident was appointed to advise the Sultan of Perak.

37 From the 1870s onwards there was peaceful co-operation between the native peoples and the Imperial Power. The State Council, one of which is shown below, became the principal instrument of the administration.

38 Sir Hugh Low, Resident of Perak from 1877 to 1889, was an outstanding success amongst British administrators. Residents brought their families, attitudes and ways of life with them into the tropics.

39 Financial reforms included an effective and just means of collecting local taxation. Here a district officer collects land rent in the village.

40 The British encouraged Chinese immigration for labour. Coaling in Singapore was typical of Chinese coolie work.

41 Tamil immigrants were employed on the rubber estates, an industry introduced by the British. The Malayan Labour Code had special reference to the welfare of Tamil labourers.

42 The Chinese looked after themselves, forming Associations (Kongsi) – the Georgetown building of one is shown here – for mutual security.

43 A demonstration of a number of Chinese Associations in Penang. By the 1920s the Chinese population in Malaya was over a million.

44 The provision of Tamil schools such as this was compulsory on the estates where there were ten or more Tamil children.

5   Malaya achieves Independence

THE GREAT DRIVING FORCE in the twentieth century Far East is nationalism – the consciousness of belonging to a racial-cultural group and the determination to preserve it. It came into being in opposition to the control of the Colonial Powers, but assumed a practical significance only after Japan's defeat of Russia in 1905 had demonstrated that an Asian country, with modern armament and discipline, could take on a European Power in war and defeat it. Nevertheless many years were to pass before this new militant nationalism could wax strong enough to challenge the West – or for that matter, the 'imperialism' of an Asian Japan.

Nationalism first reached Malaya in the form of Chinese national-ism. The latter had been born (or re-born, if the Taiping Rebellion can be taken as an antecedent) as a popular movement during the Boxer uprising in 1900 and had gained ground after the Revolution of 1911. The eventual triumph of the Kuomintang (KMT) from 1927 onwards meant that nationalism now became the main plank in Chinese policy. The KMT has adopted the 'Three Principles' of Sun Yat-sen as its doctrine, and of these the first was 'Nationalism'. Interpreted in law this meant, in effect, 'Once a Chinese, always a Chinese' through the male line for ever. This law conflicted with the nationality laws of a number of Southeast Asian countries and led to a collision between their Governments and the KMT.

The nationalism of the KMT was an important factor in stimu-lating the growth of the local Nationalisms, though in Malaya the development of a Malay nationalism was very slow. In fact, before the Second World War it had scarcely come into being. A main reason was the plural nature of Malayan society and the feeling of a need for British protection against the rapidly growing Chinese community. The decentralization policy of the 1930s and the building up of the influence of the Malay aristocracy in the Malay states encouraged the Malay nationalist intelligentsia to regard itself as the instrument for preserving an inherited culture not strong enough to stand unaided.

Chinese nationalism was challenged by Chinese Communism in the 1930s. It appealed to the 'Malayan People' to ignore nationalism and to stand together against 'Imperialism'. But then and afterwards this appeal to common class interests was less powerful than the sentiment of racial and cultural division and separation of racial interests.

Indian nationalism in Malaya was only a reflection of that of the Indian National Congress, and Malayan Indians showed little interest in local politics in pre-Second World War days.

On the eve of the Japanese war of 1941, the British were still very firmly in the saddle in Malaya. Chinese Nationalism and Communism they were able to keep under control, and the Malays showed no disposition to dispense with or weaken British protection.

The war and the Japanese occupation changed the situation beyond recognition. The military defeat for the time being marked the end of British prestige in Asia. During their occupation the Japanese cultivated the Malays, hoping to exploit their fear and resentment of Chinese pressures; the Chinese they regarded as their enemies and the Chinese Communists as enemies to be exterminated. Those Chinese Communists who escaped their massacres made their way to the forested highlands of Central Malaya where they formed a guerilla army to oppose the Japanese – but more importantly, to work for a revolution against all 'imperialism', including that of the British, should the latter return. In the last stages of the war, however, they entered into an agreement with Lord Mountbatten, the Supreme Allied Commander, whereby, in return for money and supplies, they undertook to assist the Allies in their intended invasion of Malaya to oust the Japanese.

As it turned out, the Japanese surrendered, and an invasion of Malaya was unnecessary. But when the British returned in September 1945 they found that the guerillas (which meant in effect the Malayan Communist Party which directed them) though nominally 'Allies' were in fact planning to replace them as the rulers of Malaya as soon as they were strong enough. Indeed for a time, by causing mass strikes and otherwise obstructing the British Military Administration, they very nearly succeeded in their aim. But the British were able to persuade the Malayan People's Anti-Japanese Army (MPAJA), to disband, and by taking effective action against the hidden Communist leaders to defeat their attempt to make the British position untenable. After a set-back in February 1946, when the Communists attempted to call a countrywide stoppage to celebrate the British surrender to the Japanese on 15 February 1942, they went underground, confining themselves to the infiltration of labour. But in June 1948 they came out in open rebellion against the Malayan Governments.

In the meantime there had been some important political developments. While the war was still on, the British Government had decided that as a preliminary measure towards self-government when Malaya was liberated all of the mainland of the Peninsula, including the Malay states and Penang and Malacca, should be amalgamated as a 'Malayan Union', while Singapore remained a separate British Colony. To enable this to be done, new treaties had to be made with the Rulers, and a special commissioner, Sir Harold MacMichael, was appointed to negotiate them. This he succeeded in doing, and the Malayan Union came into being on 1 April 1946 on the termination of the military government.

Under the constitution of the Union, the Rulers were reduced to a purely honorary position as presidents of religious councils. But resentment against these measures, coupled with the old fear of the Chinese, had resulted in a mass protest among the Malays which marked the birth of a genuine nationalist movement. Seeing that the introduction of the Union (however necessary as a move to political unity in place of the nine pre-war governments of an area the size of England) had been premature, the British Government decided to replace the Union by a Federation in which the Rulers had more power than at any time since British intervention in the 1870s.

The short-lived Malayan Union of 1946–48 represented in principle the unity which post-independence Malaya is seeking to attain. The greatest mistake was to make it a *fait accompli* before it had been discussed with the several communities of Malaya, especially the Malays. The Union erred also in its drastic removal of the pre-war powers of the Rulers, reducing them to the status of chairmen of religious committees while preserving to them on paper their honours and dignities. In a democracy it was inevitable that their powers should become largely nominal – but Malaya was not yet a democracy, and the prestige of the princely class was greater than citizens of European countries can easily comprehend.

The Federal Constitution of 1948 restored to – or conferred on – the sultans more powers than they had possessed since the 'Resident' system was introduced, and it was clear that when representative government was established there would again be an invasion of their prerogatives – this time from below. But the authors of the Constitution of independent Malaya were determined to preserve the mystique of princedom and the Rulers (the sultans of the seven Malay states, the Yang di-Pertuan Besar of Negri Sembilan, and the Raja of Perlis) were called upon to elect a Yang di-Pertuan Agong, a supreme Head of State, or King, who should be the constitutional monarch. He holds office for a period of five years, and is now also the Head of State of Malaysia.

Even Singapore, a self-governing Colony (now a state in the Malaysian Federation) whose population was largely Chinese, chose to accept a Malay Head of State to be known as the Yang di-Pertuan Negara. This was a significant token of a desire to be 'Malayan' on the part of the Chinese.

It had been expected that the liberation would be followed by the formation of genuine Malayan political parties. And this, after some delay, was what came about. The Malay Nationalist Party formed at the end of 1945 by Dr Burhanuddin, aimed at the inclusion of Malaya in Indonesia, but this at the time was unacceptable to Malay opinion, and the United Malays National Organization (UMNO), founded by Dato Onn bin Ja'afar to express Malay resentment against the Union, proved to be the nucleus of the nationalist move ment. The Malayan Democratic Union (MDU), in an effort to offset the influence of UMNO, formed a federation of all parties that opposed the UMNO programme (which can be simplified as 'Malaya for the Malays'). This included, in addition to the MDU, the Malayan Nationalist Party (MNP), the Pan Malayan Federation of Trade Unions, the Malayan Indian Congress (MIC), the MPAJA Old Comrades Association, the Malayan New Demo cratic Youth, the Angkatan Wanita Sedara (Women's Party), and the Angkatan Permuda Insaf (API – Youth Party). The federation called itself the All Malayan Council of Joint Action (AMCJA). Its six objectives were the unity of all Malaya including Singapore, a fully representative elected legislature, equal political rights for all who regarded Malaya as their real home and the object of their loyalty, the assumption by the Malay Sultans of the position of fully sovereign and constitutional rulers, the control of Mohammedan affairs and matters affecting Malay custom to be in the hands of the Malays, and, lastly, the encouragement of the advancement of the Malay community.

This collection of strange bed fellows did not last long. The MNP with the API seceded from AMCJA to form a Malay Council of Joint Action, and this was followed by the creation of yet another front, namely the Pusat Tenaga Ra'ayat (People's United Front) or Putera, comprising the main party of MNP, a youth organization, a woman's organization, and many smaller bodies. The leading spirit in this new creation was Dr Burhanuddin, the founder of the MNP. AMCJA was thought to be Chinese dominated and Chinese financed, while PUTERA ostensibly represented anti UMNO Malay feeling and was guided, no doubt, by the ideas of its founder.

Thus by the middle of 1948 the Malayan political scene was one of great complexity. The several forces of racial and class interest were manoeuvring for position and it was still uncertain whether they could arrange their differences and arrive at a compromise which would allow of a practical political programme. Then, in

June, when the Communists came out in rebellion, a state of emergency was declared, and regulations were brought in restricting political activity. In the changed situation, the new parties ceased to operate. AMCJA, based on the trade/unions but under Com/munist influence, broke up, while PUTERA, though it kept clear of Communist associations, felt itself powerless to make any headway.

The actual origin of the plans for the Communist uprising is still obscure. It has often been stated that it was at the Second Congress of the Communist Party of India, held under cover of the Calcutta Youth Festival in February 1948, that the rising was decided upon. But this has yet to be factually established. The outbreak in June was really only an accentuation of the violence and lawlessness that was already sporadic. Reports began to come in of shooting violence, and loss of life on estates in the Federation. On 12 June three KMT leaders were shot in daylight in Johore, on 15 June three European planters were killed on estates in Perak, and thereafter such incidents were frequent.

The civil war, which continued to be known, somewhat euphemistically, as the 'Emergency', went on for no less than twelve years. The number of Communist guerillas in the jungle was never more than 4–5,000, though this represented the optimum number for this kind of warfare and by no means the full resources of Com/munist man/power. Casualties were immediately made up by reinforcements. Something like 99 per cent of the guerillas were Chinese, with only a few Malays and Indians. The Malayan People's Liberation Army (MPLA), as they now called themselves, received their many supporters from the half million or so Chinese 'squatters' in the countryside.

The Communists were opposed by a considerable force of British and Malay troops, and about 60,000 Malay police and (later) about 40,000 Home Guard. These perfected themselves by degrees in the difficult art of jungle fighting, but the guerillas by their 'hit and run' tactics and because they could find immediate cover in the almost impenetrable Malay jungle, always had the tactical advantage. Moreover, they were always able to terrorize the people of the countryside of whatever race into supplying them with food, etc. – though a large proportion of the Chinese squatters willingly assisted them. To deny this aid to the rebels the Government decided in 1950 to resettle all the squatters into new villages over which control could be exercised so that the Communists would be denied supplies and manpower. Although this policy worked with varying degrees of success, it proved in the long run to be the key to the defeat of the Communist insurrection. The idea was that of a committee of civil servants appointed in 1948 by the High Commissioner, Sir Henry Gurney, and it was put into operation under the direction of General Sir Harold Briggs.

It can readily be appreciated that this resettlement, being a compulsory measure, had to be carried out with great tact and discretion unless the squatters were to be rendered hostile and unco-operative. They must be made to feel that the change was in their interest. This involved long-term planning, the provision of piped water and other amenities, of suitable land for cultivation, and many incidental problems. Quite apart from the requirements of the 'Emergency', this resettlement had become necessary because the Chinese squatters were a new community brought into being by the Japanese occupation; they had often 'squatted' on the Malay Reservations, had caused erosion by their gardens indiscriminately carved out of the hillsides, and had generally upset the Malayan agricultural economy. Any coercion or untactful handling would be fatal to the scheme. It was inevitable that some hardship should be caused to the villagers, but on the whole the resettlement of the 500,000 squatters was carried out with expedition and success.

The progress of the jungle war at various stages has been made actual to the general reader in the many books by British soldiers who participated in it. It was a grim and heart-breaking business calling for almost superhuman endurance as well as the highest courage and resourcefulness. It was natural and inevitable that the soldier should see the political situation in simple terms, and since the enemy were practically all Chinese, the British soldier with no previous experience of the country was bound to regard all Chinese as enemies. Such a blanket conclusion, however, would have been fatal to the British cause had it been adopted by the administration, since getting a majority of the Chinese of Malaya on to the Government's side – or at least ensuring their *neutrality* – was the secret of a successful outcome to the death struggle.

In October 1951, the High Commissioner, Sir Henry Gurney, was ambushed and murdered by Communists while on his way up to Fraser's Hill in an ordinary, unarmoured car. The question then arose as to who was to be his successor. A Conservative Government was in power in Britain, and the Colonial Secretary was Mr Oliver Lyttelton (later Lord Chandos). Lord Chandos tells us in his *Memoirs* that it was he who decided to appoint a soldier to succeed Sir Henry Gurney, and to take charge not only of the civil government but of the military operations as well. There may well have been some justification for this course in the existing situation, though the problem was (as Mr Lyttelton realized) primarily a political one.

The new High Commissioner and Commander-in-Chief, General Sir Gerald Templer, arrived in Malaya early in 1952 furnished with a 'directive' from the Secretary of State for the Colonies which instructed him to introduce legislation that would pave the way to self-government for Malaya and eventually to independence. But the rate of advance towards those objectives was apparently to be so gradual that they might be reached somewhere about the millennium. Whatever the motive may have been, the suspicion aroused was that the British intended to remain in the saddle indefinitely.

Regarding the success of the Templer regime (1952–4) in its military aspects, there existed a difference of opinion between the British and Malayan Governments. The British view was that 'General Templer, and he alone, turned the tide of the Emergency'. 'His mass punishments were not a system' (says the official statement), 'were few in number and never imposed except when it was well established that they were thoroughly deserved.' As against this, critics of the régime point out that while it is true that the General's forceful personality helped to boost European morale, this advantage was more than offset by the effects of his collective punishment on the new Chinese villages, which increased enmity towards the British without effectively denying men or food to the guerillas. The General would arrive at a village with his squadron of eight armoured cars, summon the inhabitants on parade, abuse them for helping the Communists, cut their rice ration, and then rumble off. Directly he had gone the guerillas would come out of the jungle and execute anyone who had had the temerity to obey his orders or in any way attempted to co-operate with him. Razing a village to the ground (as was on one occasion done by the General's orders), was even less conciliatory a measure than cutting a rice ration and no more effective. When the General left Malaya in 1954 there were still as many Communists active in the jungle as when he arrived two years earlier, and the rebellion still had six years to run. As Tunku Abdul Rahman, the first Prime Minister of the independent Federation, said in December 1961: 'When we took over with independence in 1957, the Communists had been claiming to be fighting for Malayan freedom. But once we had our freedom the argument lost its force, and by 1960 we were able to end the emergency.'

Meanwhile, in the intervals between his armoured forays, General Templer was carrying out the Colonial Secretary's 'directive'. One of the measures he introduced in obedience to it was a law creating 'State nationality', whereby Perlis, which had no more than 70,000 inhabitants, became endowed with a 'nationality'. (As a citizen of Wigan might say in similar circumstances 'I am not an *Englishman*; I am a *Wiganese*.') But while a measure such as this could scarcely be counted as an advance towards the creation of a 'Malayan nationality' (an avowed objective of British policy) some of the other legislation did register some progress. One measure was the admission of Non-Malay Asians into the Civil Service. There was also to be some extension of representative government by means of a Local Councils Ordinance, but in this the intention seemed to be to maintain the District Officer as the agent of the Central Government and to make him the real controller of the local councils – scarcely a 'democratic' reform. But it would be hard to convict Lord Chandos of any wildly democratic intentions; it was not 'in the blood'. When General Templer reviled Asian politicians and journalists, calling them 'dogs' and 'rats', Lord Chandos sent him a telegram of congratulation (*Memoirs*, p. 382). There was no disposition on Lord Chandos's part prematurely to surrender 'white' prestige.

The proscription of some political parties after the Emergency was declared and the fading out of others had meant that the only political organ active in the Federation was UMNO. This left a large void as far as the Chinese were concerned, and in February 1949, Mr Tan Cheng-Lock (afterwards Sir Cheng-Lock Tan) formed the Malayan Chinese Association with himself as President. The advent of the MCA was welcomed by the then High Commissioner, Sir Henry Gurney.

At the same time a Communities Liaison Committee was formed at the inspiration of the British Commissioner-General in Southeast Asia, Mr Malcolm MacDonald, to bring together the leaders of the Malay, Chinese, Indian, Ceylonese, and European communities. In January 1951, the Federal Legislative Council approved in principle the introduction of a ministerial form of government, under which there would be nine members holding portfolios who would have, in relation to the High Commissioner, the same status as ministers in other countries. This became known as the *Member System*, and was intended as a kind of emergency measure to extend representative government. (Actually it led to complications of the administration without satisfying any urge to democracy and Lord Chandos rightly abolished it.)

There was no other notable development until the formation on 20 August 1951, of the Independence of Malaya Party (IMP) under Dato Onn, who ratified the presidency of UMNO in order to start this new venture. At the outset it looked as if IMP might be a party to which the members of all communities could belong in complete equality. But the experiment was premature, and it was soon clear that Dato Onn could not carry his own child, UMNO, with him. He was succeeded in the presidency of UMNO by Tunku Abdul Rahman, under whose leadership it became an effective instrument in working towards Malayan independence.

As the Emergency continued, the feeling between the Malays and Chinese became worse and worse. This was quite understandable in the light of the fact that the Communist guerillas in the jungle were 99 per cent Chinese and that the Malays, as soldiers, homeguard, or police had to take the brunt of their attack and sustained grievous casualties. It looked on the face of it as if the breach could only widen and that it would be safe and politic for the Government to side with the Malays against the Chinese. Indeed, there is evidence to show that this is how General Templer saw the situation. Nevertheless a development was in process which made this an erroneous assumption.

The fact was that UMNO and the MCA had begun to come to an understanding whereby they would work together for indepen- dence. In October 1952, the *Manchester Guardian* correspondent in Malaya reported that tension between the Malays and the Chinese was now greater than it had been for two years, yet at this very moment a rapprochement had been taking place for some time and the two races were closer than they had ever been before.

The rapprochement began on the municipal level. This took the form early in 1952 of an UMNO–MCA Alliance to contest the elections on the basis of support for one another's Malay or Chinese candidates. The agreement could, to a great extent, be traced to the personal influence of Colonel (Tun Sir) H. S. Lee. The result was an outstanding victory for the Alliance at Kuala Lumpur, followed by successes in other municipalities, and an accord was soon reached for the extension of the Alliance to the arena of high politics.

By the beginning of 1954, it was clear from the UMNO–MCA demands that the Alliance expected a far quicker advance towards self-government than was visualized in Lord Chandos's 'directive'. What the Alliance asked for, in fact, was a constitution with a legislature with an unofficial majority.

Faced with this demand, General Templer had appointed a Federal Elections Committee *consisting of members of the Legislature itself*. No surer method could have been adopted to make certain that the recommendations would be *against* an unofficial majority, since institutions are notoriously prone to perpetuate themselves in their own image. And so it proved. The report of the Federal Elections Committee published on 1 February 1954 recommended that the present wholly official or nominated council should not be replaced immediately by a wholly elected body. A majority would be satisfied with 44 elected as against 40 nominated members, but a minority (composed largely of UMNO-MCA Alliance members and their supporters) wanted three-fifths of the council to be elected, without which, they said, responsible party government would be impossible.

After this, events moved swiftly. In April 1954 a deputation of the UMNO-MCA Alliance, headed by Tunku Abdul Rahman and Mr T.H. Tan, went to London to press the Alliance demands. Mr Lyttelton refused to meet them. Later on he changed his mind, but refused their demands. The consequence was that on the return of the deputation to Malaya, all UMNO-MCA members in the Legislative Council and serving on official boards and committees walked out in protest, and the Government was seriously handi-capped in carrying on the administration. Then, after a while, the British Government reconsidered its decision and agreed to a legislature which would have 52 elected members and 47 official and nominated members. Therefore, in order to have a majority of 5 over the official and nominated members any party or coalition of parties which aimed to form a government would have to win all of the 52 seats.

When the first elections were held on 27 July 1955, the Alliance Party (as it was now called) won 51 seats and the Pan-Malayan Islamic Party 1 seat. With a majority of four over the officials, the Alliance Party now formed a government to work for independence. In October 1954, Mr Lennox-Boyd succeeded Mr Lyttelton as Colonial Secretary, and he did everything in his power to facilitate the process to independence. In January and February 1956, agree-ments were reached between the British Government, the Malay Rulers, and the Alliance Party forming the basis of the new con-stitution. On 31 August 1957 the Federation of Malaya became the eleventh sovereign member-state of the Commonwealth of Nations.

It was indeed fortunate for Britain, Malaya, and the Common⸗
wealth that the British Government saw the 'red light' just in time. If
they had hung on indefinitely, the British would have shared the fate
of the Dutch in Indonesia and the French in Indochina. As it was they
now had Malaya as a friendly co⸗member of the Commonwealth,
and moreover continued to enjoy the advantages of the trade with
Malaya and Malaya's membership of the sterling area.

Singapore is geographically and economically part of Malaya, and
the decision taken by the British Government during the Japanese
occupation of 1942–5 to keep it as a separate Colony after liberation
led to political stresses and strains.

In April 1946, at the end of the British military government and
the resumption of the civil government, plans were put into operation
for granting Singapore a certain measure of popular representation.
Since, however, the elections held in 1948 were based on a restricted
franchise and the constitution preserved an official majority in the
legislature, they were boycotted by the local Chinese electors.
However, at the elections held in 1951, the Progressives, who had
secured a majority in 1948, were opposed by the Labour Party,
which had a programme based on that of the British Labour Party
and which demanded immediate union with the Federation. Out
of the 9 seats to be filled by election, the Progressives gained 6,
Labour 2, and the Independents 1. But out of about 300,000 persons
qualified to vote, only about 20,000 actually went to the polls.

The British Government, feeling that the extension of democratic
government must proceed more slowly in the Federation because of
the treaties with the Rulers and the delicate balance of power between
the Communities, had decided to make Singapore the testing ground
for experimental advance. Now, in view of the indifference of the
Singapore populace to the existing constitution, the British Govern⸗
ment in 1953 appointed a commission headed by Sir George Rendel
to recommend a new constitution. The commission in due course
recommended a legislature with 25 elected members out of a total of
32. Six of the elected members were to be members of a Council
of Ministers replacing the Executive Council, the Chambers of

Commerce were to be deprived of political representation; and the names of those entitled to vote would automatically be included in the registers. Brought into operation in 1955, those measures led to a vote of more than 50 per cent of the new electorate.

Small as the Singapore parties were, they were subject to further fragmentation. A schism had taken place in the Labour Party in 1954 when one faction had formed the Labour Front with the newly-established Socialist Party. Then, in November 1959, still further to the Left, the People's Action Party (PAP) made its appearance, led by Mr Lee Kuan-Yew, which had the support of the Trade Unions. Mr Lee Kuan-Yew was an English-speaking Hakka Chinese, who took a 'starred' first in law at Cambridge. At this time he enjoyed the support of the Chinese trade unions, but as time went on the Communist influence in the Unions became greater with consequences that were detrimental to the PAP. But this development only became apparent under the next (the third) Singapore constitution. At the elections of 2 April 1955, of 25 seats the Labour Front obtained 10, the Progressives 4, the PAP and the Alliance Party (a branch of the party of that name in the Federation) 3 each, the Democrats 2, and the Independents 3.

There was no single party with a sufficient majority to form a government, but the leader of the Labour Front, Mr David Marshall, was able to do so with the assistance of the Alliance Party. He was immediately faced with difficulties – internally from strikes and agitation among the pupils of the Chinese secondary schools (as always, 'Leftist', and demonstrating for the pre-eminence of education in the Chinese language), and externally, over the future relationship between Singapore and the British Government. Since the Federation was now proceeding rapidly towards independence with the blessing of the British Government, it was inevitable that Singapore should wish to do the same. In August 1955, the Secretary of State for the Colonies, Mr Lennox-Boyd, visited Singapore and consultations took place between him and the Chief Minister. Difficulties arose over the provisions of the proposed new constitution for security, but on his return to London the Colonial Secretary announced that in the event of the suspension of the constitution by the British Government for security reasons the Governor of Singapore would nevertheless act in conformity with the recommendations of the Chief Minister. He thus recognized the existence of a parliamentary government, and that the following year negotiations would be opened in London on the question of self-government for Singapore.

Negotiations duly opened in London the following April but foundered on the rock of 'military security'. The British Government would agree to recognize internal sovereignty only on condition that the constitution might be suspended in a situation where the contemplated Committee of Security and Defence considered it impossible for the High Commissioner (the British official who would replace the Governor) to carry out his responsibility as regards defence and external affairs. On this point there was a complete deadlock, and on his return to Singapore Mr Marshall resigned as Chief Minister. He was replaced by another member of the Labour Front, Mr Lim Yew-Hock, a Malayan Chinese, who reopened the negotiations with Britain the following year. In March 1957 a new conference was called and this time agreement was reached. The Defence Committee, it was now agreed, should consist of three British Representatives (with the High Commissioner as Chairman), three Singapore Ministers, and a representative of the Federation who should have the casting vote. The legislative assembly would consist of 51 members, elected by the universal suffrage of all adults, male and female, on a common roll irrespective of community. The Queen's Representative was to be a Malayan Yang di-Pertuan Negara, a Head of State.

Under the new constitution, the self-governing state of Singapore came into being at midnight on 2–3 June 1959. The first elections had been held on 30 May at which the People's Action Party, under Mr Lee Kuan-Yew, won an overwhelming victory. Of the 51 seats, 43 were won by PAP, 4 by the Singapore People's Alliance under Lim Yew-Hock, 3 by UMNO – MCA (Alliance), and 1 by an Independent. Mr Lee Kuan-Yew and his party were committed to a programme that was 'Anti-Colonial' and decidedly to the 'Left', but making a great feature of coming to terms with the Malays of the

Federation. Malay was to be accepted as the official language of Singapore.

Thus, as the fifth decade of the twentieth century moved on to its close, we see an independent Federation in being and getting to grips with the problems of independence, and a self-governing Singapore faced with the question as to the form its own independence should take when the time came, which would in all probability be in 1963, when the constitution of 1959 was due for reconsideration. Should it be independent on its own, as part of the Federation of Malaya, as a state in federal association with Malaya, or as a unit in a larger federation or confederation which would embrace the other territories in the region at present still under British control? What this decision was, and how it was made will be considered in another chapter, but first of all we must outline the course of post-independence politics in the Federation, adding simultaneous developments in Singapore.

45   The elephant was once the only means of jungle land transport in Malaya.

46 Road constrution called for cosiderable engineerinskill.

47-48 The firsrailway lines, opened in the 1880s, linked the tin mining centres in westcentral Malaya.

49 Sugar was an important agricultural product in the second half of the nineteenth century but declined after the abolition of indentured labour in 1910. The last sugar factory closed in 1913.

50 The Malays are traditionally a sea-faring people. Fishing remains particularly important on the east coast.

51 The Chinese pioneered tin mining and for many years held a virtual monopoly.

52 A primitive Chinese tin-ore smelting furnace

53 More effi
mining method
cluding the
dredge shown
required cap
beyond the reso
of the Chin
Gradually the
dustry passed
European hands

54 Pinnacle
limestone rock
after the tin has
dredged. Abou
per cent of Mal
mining today i
tin. (right)

55 In 1897 only 345 acres were under rubber but within fifty years the acreage had risen to over 3 million. Western large-scale production techniques dominated the industry. A small Malay plantation is shown here.

56 A simple process is required to turn the latex into sheets, which are a common sight hanging outside village dwellings.

57 Two-thirds of all rubber comes from the plantations of large estates, such as this British-owned one. (*top right*)

58 Modern smoke-houses are geared for massive rubber production. (*right*)

59 Planting out rubber seedlings. The rubber plant has its origins in South America. Henry Ridley experimented in Singapore with saplings shipped from Kew Gardens, London, and it is on his work that Malaya's rubber industry is based.

6   Malaya since Independence

TO UNDERSTAND THE INTERNAL POLITICS of Malaya, it is also necessary to have some appreciation of the country's external relations. This was particularly the case in the 1960s because Communist China was looming so large in the Far East and nearly half of Malaya's population was Chinese, but it was also true that Malaya was subject to other pulls and pressures due to having Indonesia as a near neighbour. Again, the world military organiza/ tion in the Cold War and the existence of defence treaties affecting the Southeast Asian region had a decided influence on Malayan politics both internal and external.

The twelve-year long battle with the Chinese Communist guerillas in the jungle had left behind a legacy of suspicion in the minds of the Malays. The People's Government of China had given moral support to the insurgents on the pretext that they represented the 'Malayan people', irrespective of race, in arms against Western 'imperialism', whereas, as we have seen, 99 per cent of them were Chinese. Moreover, there was no guarantee that the Chinese Communists would not come out again in rebellion against the independent Government of Malaya as soon as the opportunity offered, and the danger spot this time for a new outbreak seemed to be Singapore where the Communists were very active in the trade-unions. Thus the Alliance Government showed definite hostility towards People's China, refusing to give it diplomatic recognition (although Britain was in diplomatic relations with it), and, on the ground that the dumping of Communist goods in Malaya was injuring Malayan economy, also refusing to allow the People's Bank of China to open a branch in the Federation.

It was this same feeling of fear and resentment of Communist China which caused the Prime Minister, Tunku Abdul Rahman, to side warmly with India over the Sino–Indian frontier war which reached its climax in 1962.

Yet, although the Southeast Asia Treaty Organization (SEATO) was designed to defend Southeast Asia from any external attack, which in the circumstances could only come from China, Malaya refused to join it. It wanted no involvements of this sort. At the same time Malaya had entered into a military treaty with Britain, whereby Britain maintained forces in Malaya to help prevent another Communist rising and to defend her from external attack. These forces were not to be regarded as part of the SEATO forces and no SEATO operations were to be carried out from bases in the Federation.

Meanwhile, Malaya's trade was with the West and the largest markets for Malayan rubber and tin were the United States and Europe. Also, Malaya, in order to develop its resources, had need of more foreign capital and this again could come only from the West.

The economic structure of Malaya had a bearing, too, on the attitude of the Malayan Chinese. The MCA could be said to be 'conservative' in the sense that it proposed no radical change in Malaya's economy, and the interests of Chinese merchants and retailers were largely tied up with the Western trade system. Even those Chinese trade-unionists in Singapore with Communist leanings had to reflect on Singapore's vulnerability to indiscriminate strike action, depending on the Federation for the bulk of its export trade and even for its water supply as it was. Besides, nearly all Singapore's food had to be imported.

Between the Malayan Alliance Government and the neighbouring Thailand there was no important difference, but the proximity of Indonesia did pose a problem. On the whole, the Indonesian ministers had abstained from making any direct claims for the inclusion of Malaya or the British Borneo territories as part of Indonesia, but those claims were voiced by some Indonesian politicians and inside Malaya itself. The Pan-Malayan Islamic Party (PMIP), led by Dr Burhanuddin, made this aim a major plank in their platform. But UMNO were firmly opposed to any such plan.

On achieving independence, the Federation became a member of the Commonwealth, and as such took up a position strongly opposed to *Apartheid* in South Africa in the debate which finally led to the withdrawal of the Union of South Africa from the Commonwealth.

It is against this international background that Malaya's post-independence politics must be reviewed. At the same time we shall have to bear in mind the sharp differentiation between the three principal communities, the Malays, the Chinese, and the Indians and Pakistanis. Moreover, there were marked regional differences. The large urban population and that of the more important tin-areas was predominantly Chinese. Rubber plantations owned by European companies usually employed Indian labour, whereas plantations owned by Chinese were usually worked by Chinese labourers. Rubber small-holdings, which accounted for a substantial pro-portion of the aggregate Malayan production of rubber, were mostly owned by Malays and Chinese and worked by the tenants and their families. Malays formed the majority of the population in the important rice-growing areas (e.g. in Kedah and Kelantan) and fishing was almost exclusively a Malay occupation on the east coast of Malaya.

Having led Malaya triumphantly to independence, the Alliance had now to consider how best it might ensure its own political future.

As we know, the Alliance won 51 out of the 52 seats to be filled by voting at the 1955 elections. Their candidates obtained approxi-mately 80 per cent of the total votes cast, and in each of the 51 constituencies in which the Alliance was successful their candidate obtained more than twice as many votes as any of his rivals. The only seat lost by the Alliance was where a three-cornered fight occurred in the Krian constituency of Perak, with the Pan-Malayan Islamic Party candidate finishing just ahead of the Alliance candidate and a candidate from the National Association of Perak a rather poor third. In 1955 the Alliance was the only party adequately organized for a general election.

At these 1955 elections only the Party Negara (led by Dato Onn bin Ja'afar, the founder of UMNO, and stressing Malay rights) contested more than half the seats, but its efforts were unsuccessful and 13 of its 30 candidates lost their deposits. There were 11 PMIP candidates whose main objective was a Pan-Malayan Islamic State, 3 in Kelantan, 3 in Perak, 2 in Selangor, and 1 each in Kedah, Pahang, and Penang; 2 of the 3 candidates in Kelantan, 1 of the 3 in Perak and the single Kedah and Pahang candidates lost their deposits (it is worth remarking that Tunku Abdul Rahman, the Prime Minister, belonged to the Kedah royal family and had mass support among the Kedah Malays). The geographical distribution of the PMIP candidates and their fortunes at the 1955 elections will be of considerable interest when we come to consider the results of the 1959 elections.

Subsequent to the 1955 elections, the National Association of Perak and the Perak Malay League went out of existence and the Labour Party joined the Party Ra'ayat to form the Socialist Front. The extreme left-wing Perak Progressive Party became the People's Progressive Party; its sphere of influence lay largely inside the state of Perak.

Now, at the 1955 elections, the electorate of 1,280,000 persons was very largely Malay. This was because of the operation of the citizenship laws passed during the British period which gave citizenship automatically to Malays and other Malaysians and to other races only on certain conditions. It was estimated that some 84 per cent of the electorate were Malay, 11 per cent Chinese, and the remaining 5 per cent mainly Indian. In 1959, when the first elections under independence were held, the electorate had increased from 1,280,000 to 2,177,000 and the proportion of non-Malay electors was very considerably larger than in 1955. The 1959 electorate was estimated to contain 750,000 Chinese as compared with under 150,000 in 1955. Approximately 57 per cent of the increased electorate was Malay, 36 per cent Chinese and 7 per cent Indian. The constitution of independent Malaya had made it easier to obtain citizenship by registration or naturalization, and special concessions were made during the first twelve months after the Federation became

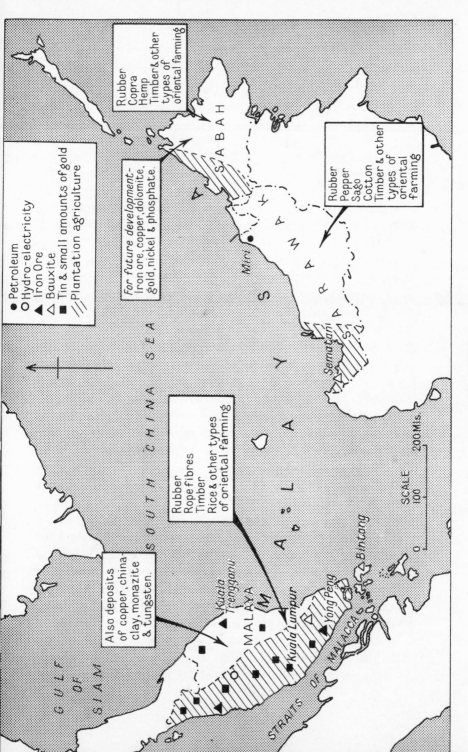

Economic map of Malaysia

Legend:
- ● Petroleum
- ○ Hydro-electricity
- ▲ Iron Ore
- △ Bauxite
- ■ Tin & small amounts of gold
- /// Plantation agriculture

Rubber
Copra
Hemp
Timber & other types of oriental farming

Rubber
Pepper
Sago
Cotton
Timber & other types of oriental farming

For future development—
Iron ore, copper, dolomite.
gold, nickel & phosphate.

Rubber
Rope fibres
Timber
Rice & other types of oriental farming

Also deposits of copper, china clay, monazite & tungsten.

SCALE
0   100   200 Mls.

SOUTH CHINA SEA

GULF OF SIAM

STRAITS OF MALACCA

SABAH
SARAWAK
MALAYA
Miri
Sematan
Kuala Trengganu
Kuala Lumpur
Yong Peng
Bintang

independent in 1957. (See 'The Malayan Elections of 1959', by T. E. Smith, *Pacific Affairs*, March 1960.)

The Alliance was based on an agreement between the Malays and the Chinese as represented by their respective organizations. This agreement in turn was based on a tacit understanding – and one that was unlikely to be expressed in writing at any time. This was a recognition that the interests of Malays and Chinese were quite distinct, as were both from those of the Indians, whose MIC had now joined the Alliance Party. Dato Onn's Independence of Malaya Party which contemplated a common membership of all communities had been recognized both by UMNO and the MCA to be premature (the failure to recognize this fact had brought about Dato Onn's political eclipse). But believing that they could work out a solution of their inter-communal difficulties better under independence, the two associations had combined to that end. The Malays, by virtue of the citizenship laws passed during the British period in which the principle of the 'special position of the Malays' was accepted, had a numerical superiority at the 1955 elections, and because of their inheritance from the British period the Malays otherwise enjoyed a political advantage. The Chinese, on the other hand, had the economic superiority. What then would happen after independence? Would there still be a tacit understanding that the Malays should continue to enjoy the political advantage and the Chinese the economic? On no other conditions did a continuance of the Alliance seem possible. Would there, on the other hand, be a chance that Malayan politics would develop on non-racial lines?

One inevitable consequence that flowed from the independence constitution was that there would eventually be complete equality of franchise between the races, and that was because the constitution provided for automatic citizenship, irrespective of race, for all persons born in Malaya after independence. But in the meantime, while the children were growing up, there would be an increase in the numbers of the Chinese and Indian voters by the operation of other citizenship laws. The Malays, therefore, would progressively lose their privileged political position. But was there a chance that, on the other hand, they could improve their economic position until it was comparable with that of the Chinese? The answer lay in whether schemes to improve the lot of the Malay *rayat* such as those planned by the Rural and Industrial Development Administration (RIDA) before independence would receive adequate financing from the revenues, and whether the other communities (notably the Chinese) would submit to the scale of taxation that would yield these revenues.

Before the 1959 elections, many young Chinese were restive because of the inequality of citizenship. This was reflected inside the MCA. Also for some time past, the MCA had been dissatisfied with the Government's education policy (and from time to time with other aspects of its policy), and trouble finally came to a head when the candidates for the 1959 Parliamentary elections came to be chosen. In 1955, the Alliance had chosen 35 Malays, 15 Chinese, 1 Indian, and 1 Ceylonese as candidates for the 52 seats. When the time came to choose the candidates for the 104 seats for the 1959 Parliamentary general election, UMNO the dominant member of the Alliance, wanted 75 Malay, 27 Chinese, and 2 Indian candidates to be nominated, whereas a large section of the MCA wanted at least 35 Chinese candidates. The final compromise reached was 69 candidates to UMNO, 31 to MCA and 4 to MIC. But this compromise was only just approved by the MCA and it led to the resignation of a number of members of the MCA, some of whom stood as independent candidates in opposition to the Alliance at the elections.

Even before the general elections were held, the Alliance had further trouble at the state elections. Having swept the board in Kedah and Perlis, they suffered defeats in Kelantan, where PMIP won 28 seats out of the 30 seats in the State Council and in Trengganu where PMIP won 13 seats out of the 24, against the 7 won by the Alliance and 4 by Dato Onn's Party Negara. But these were states largely populated by Malays.

At the general election, the Alliance nominated a candidate for every seat and 3 were returned unopposed. The challenge to the Alliance came from PMIP with 50 candidates, from the Socialist

Front with 37 candidates and from the People's Progressive Party with 19 candidates.

The most serious immediate challenge came from PMIP. It stood for Malaya for the Malays in an Islamic theocratic state. The party promised to 'restore' Malay sovereignty by changing the constitution and it proposed to establish friendly relations with all Muslim countries. All treaties permitting foreign troops to be stationed in Malaya were to be abolished under its manifesto. The leader of the party was Dr Burhanuddin, the founder of the MNP which had been proscribed during the Emergency. Incorporation of Malaya into Indonesia does not appear to have been included in the PMIP election pledges, but the party nevertheless looked to Indonesia for inspiration.

Party Negara was also a pro-Malay party, and took the line that the Malays had been badly let down by the existing constitution. Of its candidates, however, only Dato Onn himself was returned to Parliament. This, in fact, was to prove the political end of Dato Onn (who died in 1962). It was ironical that the founder of UMNO and the virtual creator of Malay Nationalism should have sacrificed his leadership, first by a premature attempt to establish a Malayan equal citizenship with his IMP, and secondly, by challenging the compromise between the Malays and the Chinese represented by the Alliance and attempting belatedly to take a Malay Nationalist line in competition with the extreme PMIP.

In the new Southeast Asia, Socialism had been much to the fore, and it might be expected that it would make its appearance in Malaya now that an elected legislature had made its appearance. This proved to be the case, and Socialist aims appeared in the programmes of two minor parties. One was the Socialist Front, comprising the Labour Party and the Party Ra'yat, which published a rather vague manifesto and talked about 'a planned Socialist economy'. Another was the People's Progressive Party which condemned Malay nationalism, demanded amendments to the constitution to provide equal rights and privileges irrespective of race, and opposed the existing 'Malay' bias in the educational policy (instituted by the Alliance Government). It called for school

Political map of Southeast Asia

instruction in the mother tongue of the pupil but retaining Malay as a compulsory school subject. Its Socialist aims included the nationalization of the tin and rubber industries, and a new system of taxation to benefit the lower income groups at the expense of the higher income groups. It was led by the brothers Seenivasagam (both Indian lawyers), but the non-communal and educational items in PPP's programme might be expected to appeal to Chinese dissatisfied with the Alliance.

The results of the 1959 elections were as follows. The Alliance won 74 seats (52 of its 69 Malay candidates, 19 of its 31 Chinese candidates, and 3 of its 4 Indian candidates having been successful) in Kedah, Perlis, Johore, and Pahang. In Negri Sembilan they won 4 of the 6 seats, the other two going to independent Chinese candidates who had resigned from the MCA in July. The PPP won 4 of the 20 seats in Perak, and another of the seats was won by a Chinese independent. In Penang the Socialist Front won 3 of the 8 seats and 5 of the 14 seats in Selangor, making a total of 8. The PMIP won 13 out of 16 seats in Kelantan and Trengganu. Party Negara won 1 seat only (that of Dato Onn himself) in Trengganu, and the Malayan Party (a party of purely local significance) won a seat in Malacca. The Alliance was thus back in power but with only 74 out of 104 seats as compared with 51 out of 52 seats in 1955.

These results naturally led to some speculation regarding the future pattern of politics in the Federation. If the next few years saw a continuation of the social and economic progress that had marked the first two years of independence, the narrow Malay communal parties might well fail to make any further headway. It has to be remembered, too, that the proportion of the Chinese vote was increasing at every election. The main danger to the Alliance was likely to come from the left-wing parties. It was significant that the Alliance was most unsuccessful in the constituencies in and around the larger towns in Malaya. 'In the course of the next five years (wrote Mr T. E. Smith in 1960) the Malay vote, though remaining predominant, will continue to diminish slowly in importance. The extent to which the Alliance can find a real basis for Chinese and

Indian support may therefore well determine the outcome of Malaya's next Parliamentary elections.'

In the event, at the Malayan elections of April 1964, the Alliance obtained 89 seats (as compared with 74 in 1959), and PMIP only 9 seats (15 in 1959). But the Indonesian 'confrontation' of Malaysia no doubt helped the Alliance at the polls.

The above describes in outline the basic political situation in the Federation between 1957 and 1963 (by when the Alliance Party, in fact, had improved its position), except for the situation entailed by the 'Greater Malaysia' proposals (which are discussed in chapter 8). But needless to say there were frequent events which modified the existing pattern and even at times threatened to change it. This can be indicated by a few sidelights on Malayan politics during the period.

In this Malayan plural society the enduring problem was race relationship. The Alliance itself was the outcome of a compromise and its existence could be jeopardized by extremism among either the Malay or Chinese communities. Tunku Abdul Rahman issued a warning against racialism in his message on the fourth anniversary of independence (31 August 1961).

It was clear, however, that the Tunku foresaw more danger from the communalism and Communism of the 'Left' than the extremism of the Malays of the 'Right'. This appraisal must have been strengthened when after some two years of office, the PMIP government in Trengganu was defeated and replaced by an Alliance government, and when later the Alliance won a by-election (caused by the death of Dato Onn), the UMNO candidate defeating the Party Negara by 7,275 votes to 5,148 and the PMIP candidate getting only 889 votes and losing his deposit. This was the heart of what hitherto had been PMIP territory.

From the other side of the political stage came a challenge to the Alliance in the form of the United Democratic Party under the chairmanship of Dr Lim Chong-Eu, a one-time President of the Penang MCA and a nominated member of Legislative Council before independence. The Party was pledged to fight constitutional amendments which would make citizenship more difficult for non-Malays and also to oppose the 'crash' programme to establish the Federation of Malaysia. The Party disclaimed any undemocratic action and when, in a speech at the end of April, the Prime Minister charged the UDP with weakening the MCA, and included it with the PPP and the Socialist Front as groups that were trying to wreck the Association of Southeast Asia (ASA – a somewhat theoretical federation of the future) and the proposals for Malaysia, the UDP's President appealed to the Prime Minister to adopt 'a much more paternal attitude towards the opposition parties' for the sake of parliamentary democracy and the future progress of the country. The Tunku's reference to splitting the Alliance was, he said, a travesty of the UDP's declared aims.

But the Tunku had no illusions as to who his real enemies were. They were the Communists, especially those in Singapore. Speaking at two functions in Singapore on 25 March 1962, the Tunku gave a warning that if the people of Singapore (by rejecting Communist influence) did not then decide in favour of the General Malaysia plan he would 'close the Johore causeway'. (Later on, however, he modified this threat by saying that the closing of the causeway would not affect the economic life of Malaya which would go on as usual.) The Communists (he said on another occasion) were also attempting to wreck the Association of Southeast Asia and plans for Malaysia by exploiting a 'strong Chinese characteristic element in the Federation who refuse to be Malayans in heart and spirit'. The Chinese Communist Party (he went on) was trying to influence the minds of the Malays through a strong Communist peasant movement in Indonesia. The Tunku must have had in mind, too, the fact that late in 1961 about 500 Communist guerillas were said to be still operating in the Malayan–Thai border jungle, of whom two were former Japanese soldiers who served in upper Perak during the war.

The first elections in Singapore under the new constitution for the Legislative Assembly were held on 30 May 1959, and, as we have seen, the PAP under Lee Kuan-Yew won an overwhelming victory. The PAP, however, announced that it would not take office until the release of eight of its members who had been detained by Mr Lim Yew-Hock after the riots of 1956.

As the subterranean activities of the Communists continued, the position of Mr Lee Kuan-Yew inside his own party (PAP) was more and more obviously at stake. In the Legislative Assembly in August 1960, the Prime Minister declared that a collision was bound to take place between the 'adventurers of the Left' and the 'colonialist imperialists', and that the PAP policy was to allow them to tear one another to pieces.

But although for the time being Mr Lee retained his majority in the PAP, there were signs that his leadership was threatened. One of these signs was the success at a by-election in April 1961 of his opponent, Mr Ong Eng-Guan, who had been a PAP Minister but had been compelled to resign after a personal attack on the Prime Minister. Mr Ong had come into the limelight some years before when as Mayor of Singapore he had banned the use of the civic regalia inherited from the British period and had had the Union Jack removed from the Council Chamber. On his election by 7,747 votes to the 4,927 polled by the PAP candidate, Mr Ong declared that the result was a 'triumphant victory of the people against a government that had so disappointed them'. Only two months later, a second and perhaps more serious setback for Lee Kuan-Yew was the success at another by-election of Mr David Marshall, the ex-Chief Minister under the previous constitution, with a majority of 546 over the PAP candidate, who polled 3,052.

The portents were that Mr Lee Kuan-Yew was losing the support of the trade-unions to the Communists and retained only the firm backing of the civil servants and the University, its graduates and students (the English-speaking element of the population). In the second half of 1961, he gave a long series of talks over Radio Singapore to show how the Communists had striven increasingly to gain control of PAP since its formation in 1954. He described their subterranean action and their policies.

Things went from bad to worse with PAP the following year. When Mrs How Puay-Choo resigned from the party on 2 July 1962, and became an independent member, the strength of P A P in the Legislative Assembly was reduced to 25 against a combined opposition strength of 26. The Prime Minister, however, told press reporters that 'until the opposition outvotes us we are still the constitutional Government'. And so it proved when on 13 July a three-party (Socialist Front, United People's Party, Workers Party) no-confidence motion was defeated by 24 votes to 16. The 7 Singapore People's Alliance and the UMNO-MCA Alliance members abstained from voting. This was after a very long and heated debate in which the S P A leader, Mr Lim Yew-Hock, moved an amendment to the motion with the aim of condemning the Government for its failure to restrain known Communist leaders, saying that as a responsible opposition he and his followers would 'not be deterred from voting with the Government on any issue that will mean the extermination of the Communist pest'.

In a broadcast in October 1961, Mr Lee Kuan-Yew said that the Communist attempts to force the P A P out of office were now being transferred to the industrial front. What seemed to be the first move in this direction took place on 1 November when the Public Daily-Rated Employees' Union Federation forced a strike of City Council Workers. There were a few minor outbreaks of violence; lorries were overturned or stoned, bicycles were smashed, and 13 people were hurt and 22 arrested. These incidents, however, were isolated acts of violence. Labour pressure continued and wage-claims were the order of the day. In fact, labour relations were, it seemed, the key to Singapore's future, and further foreign investment was bound to be contingent on a satisfactory *modus vivendi* between capital and labour. Labour relations in the Federation meanwhile were, in contrast to those in Singapore, outstandingly good.

Apart from the threat of direct action by the Communists, Mr Lee Kuan-Yew's principal headache was undoubtedly educational policy. This was a matter which had caused a split in Singapore society for decades. Periodically there had been strikes, boycotts and processions by the teachers and pupils of Chinese schools in Singapore directed to maintaining and extending the use of Chinese as a medium of instruction in Singapore education and to obtaining increased government financing for Chinese schools. Since Communist China was the main proponent of Chinese culture and the source of the bulk of the modern literature to which an education in Chinese gave access, the education question could not fail to have a strong political colour – however much the school or teachers might dissociate themselves from politics. But although Malay was the 'official' language of Singapore, English was still the language of administration and the Courts. The degrees of the University of Singapore were a passport to official employment while those of Nanyang University (a Chinese organization in which English was the official medium of instruction but Chinese was commonly used) had hitherto not been accepted as being of sufficiently high standard (though as we shall see in our final chapter, a change was to come). Mr Lee himself was English-educated but was endeavouring to be the mediator between the two rival camps.

Speaking in the Singapore Legislative Assembly in December 1961, the Minister for Education, Mr Yong Nyuk-Lin, said that it was clear that the boycott of Chinese Secondary School examinations was part of a Communist campaign to stir up feeling against the Government. The Communist allegations at the time had been that the PAP Government planned 'to strangle Chinese culture'. The Minister said that on 14 December seven people purporting to represent the 'All-Singapore Secondary Students' Parents' Association', had called on him, but in fact not a single one of the seven was a genuine parent of any student concerned with the examinations, and one was an ex-terrorist, Ong Ban-Song, who had deserted from his unit in the jungle and surrendered to the Security Forces in March 1954.

So while the PAP Government's local anxieties were focused on the Communists and their pressures exerted through labour or education, its attention externally was attracted by the proposals for the merger of Singapore into a larger political association. Singapore, it was clear, was not by itself a viable political unit, and its separation from the remainder of Malaya to which it belonged geographically and economically allowed internal pressure groups to exercise an influence out of proportion to their numbers and importance.

60 The outbreak of the Japanese war in 1941 marked the beginning of the end of British rule in Malaya. A street in Singapore after Japanese bombardment.

61 The surrender of the British in Singapore was a symbolic defeat by Asia of the West. Nothing could be the same again.

馬來亞人民抗日軍中央軍委會

姓名　白娜

入伍時間　一九四三年

職位　隊員（滅版部英文工作）

（蓋印）

=民族英雄=

"為人類和平正義
為民族解放
為主義殉難是
馬來亞人民抗日軍軍人
的特色風度"—萊特

永垂不朽！

62 Communists, most of them Chinese, who escaped to the central highlands founded the Malayan People's Anti-Japanese Army. An Old Comrades Association membership card is shown here, significantly with no Malay on it.

63 Only three years later British and Malay troops opposed mainly Chinese rebels in a jungle war known as the 'Emergency' which lasted for twelve years.

64 Chinese farmers, or squatters, living in isolated parts were the main economic support of the guerrillas. They had to be closely watched through frequent visits such as this one by a special constable.

65 Troops were aided in the later stages of the emergency by 40,000 Malayan home guards, some of which are seen here being trained to guard their own village.

66–67 Chinese squatters, and jungle villages were difficult to protect from the rebels. From 1950 onwards a massive scheme for resettling half a million people in new villages was carried out. The communists were thereby denied essential supplies and manpower.

8 Gradually the rebels were driven from the jungle. Although most of them are Chinese there were exceptions such as this Tamil.

9 Many people suspected of active association with the rebels were detained at rehabilitation camps. This one was at Penang.

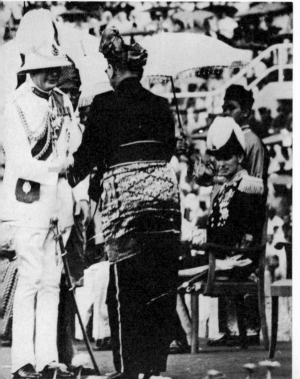

70 Chinese and Malays, although at war in the jungle, formed in civilian life a political alliance. The overwhelming victory of the Alliance Party in the elections of July 1955 was a major step towards independence.

71 On 31 August 1957, Malaya achieved independence. The Duke of Gloucester hands the independence scroll to the Prime Minister, Tunku Abdul Rahman.

72 'Merdeka' or Independence, was celebrated throughout Malaya. In the federal capital of Kuala Lumpur the biggest parade in Malayan history was held. (*top right*)

73 At midnight the Union Jack was lowered for the last time. (*right*)

74 Tunku Abdul Rahman, in traditional Malay dress, reads the oath of office as he is sworn into the Prime Ministership.

75 After independence an amnesty was offered to the communist terrorists. The Prime Minister heads a procession through Kuala Lumpur in support of it. But the war continued and the amnesty was revoked.

76 In the 1959 election the Alliance Party won a smaller proportion of seats than in the last election before independence. It has nevertheless remained the dominant party, and improved its position in the 1964 elections.

77 Eventually, in July 1960, the 'Emergency' came to an end and the proclamation revoking emergency regulations was signed.

78 In Singapore the minority administration of David Marshall formed after the elections of April 1955, lasted for a little over a year.

79 In the elections of May 1959 Lee Kuan-yew's People's Action Party won a clear victory. He made the release of eight members of his party held in Changi gaol since the riots of 1956 a condition of forming a Government. The emblem held in this demonstration outside the gaol is that of the P A P.

80   The problem of internal security was a stumbling-block to constitutional progress
in Singapore. The Chinese schools were centres of leftist activity, and tear-gas was
used by police to break up demonstrations.

81   Although a strong left winger, the new Prime Minister was obliged to take an
increasingly firm anti-communist line, faced as he was with threats of direct action,
infiltration into the unions, and strikes.

82   The prosperity of Singapore is as dependent as ever upon trade and is linked to
Malaya as its largest port, handling 90 per cent of all Malaya's entrepôt trade. This
was a powerful reason for membership of the Malaysian Federation.

7 Sarawak and Sabah

THE HUGE ISLAND OF BORNEO (the name is derived from 'Brunei'), the third largest in the world, has an area of 287,000 square miles – roughly five times as great as that of England and Wales or three times that of Michigan, USA. Yet, in spite of its size, it has always been the 'Dark Continent', so to speak, of Southeast Asia. There is evidence of many ancient Chinese contacts with the island, and of Hindu penetration along its rivers in the first millennium A.D. But for the most part it was left for many centuries to its aboriginal peoples, thinly scattered over its surface, in the hunting and food-collecting stage of development. When they practised agriculture it was of the primitive shifting type. This isolation was due to a number of factors – low fertility of much of the surface and the rare sunshine of the climate, the lack of coast-line due to the island's compactness, the difficulty of approach by the rivers which invariably had shifting bars across their mouths, that made Borneo so much less attractive to the settlers than (say) rich volcanic-soiled Java or the spice-growing Moluccas.

As recently as 1856 Crawfurd could write:

all attempts on the part of European nations to establish a permanent territorial dominion over Borneo, we may rest assured, will, in the long run be baffled by the insuperable obstacles of an uncongenial climate, a stubborn soil, a rude and intractable population, and the absence of all adequate financial resources.[11]

Since this sweeping prophecy, Borneo officials have reacted strongly, denying its truth in every respect, but the fact remains that it is only in the present century that Borneo has shown any promise of being

157

susceptible of development or of supporting a considerable population.

The island bestrides the equator, is predominantly covered with tropical rain forest, merging at altitudes into great stretches of mountain moss forest and in the coastal lowlands into freshwater swamp and mangroves. The fauna comprises a large number of species, the most remarkable of the animals being the orangutang. There are also many of the creatures which occur in Malaya (including the rhinoceros and the elephant in the north in small numbers) but the tiger is absent. The flora also is very rich, and again bears a close resemblance to that of Malaya. Throughout the island the average temperature is from 78° to 80°F., but the thermometer rarely falls below 70°, except in the hills, and occasionally on exceptional days mounts as high as 96° in the shade. In this respect once more, and in its humidity, the Borneo climate is not noticeably different from that of Malaya.

There is no doubt that Borneo's few serviceable ports were visited by foreigners from early times, but the island was never brought under administration until the arrival of the Europeans – and even then only slowly and partially. As D. G. E. Hall remarks, 'So far as ascertainable facts go, the state of Majapahit was limited to East Java, Madura and Bali', and the earlier empire of Sri Vijaya did not include Borneo in any effective way.

The conquest of Malacca by the Portuguese in 1511 deprived the Muslim traders of their main entrepôt in these waters and they then transferred their headquarters to Brunei on the northern coast of Borneo. Brunei was visited by Magellan's expedition in 1521, after the death of its leader in the Philippines, and Pigafetta, its historian, has left an animated account of the busy principality. (He does not incidentally, mention the presence of any Chinese in Brunei.) After 1526, however, Acheh in Sumatra became the leader of the opposition to the Portuguese and Brunei declined in importance although it still claimed most of the northern part of the island as its territory.

After the establishment of their power in Indonesia, the Dutch claimed Borneo as being under their sovereignty, but they concentrated their attention on Java and the Moluccas and largely ignored the great dark island in the centre of Indonesia. In the latter part of the eighteenth century (from 1760 onwards) the Chinese began a serious penetration of Western Borneo. They were attracted by gold, but they did not confine their activities to mining it. They established a systematic procedure, clearing large tracts of land, cultivating pepper, and laying out vegetable gardens. They began to ignore the local sultan of Sambas, establishing independent control of their own affairs under their Kongsis (societies), and also engaging in warfare with the Dayaks. The temporary replacement of the Dutch in Indonesia by the British from 1811 to 1816 did not greatly affect the authority of the Kongsis (since the British were preoccupied with other matters) but when the Dutch resumed their overlordship of the archipelago, under the Treaty of Vienna, they resolved to establish direct control over Borneo. Effective action was interrupted for a long period by the Great Java War, but finally Chinese obstinacy was defeated by Dutch phlegm and the year 1854 saw the complete extinction of the Kongsis.

The modern history of Borneo, however, can be said to begin in earnest with the arrival of James Brooke in Borneo and his assumption of responsibility as Raja of Sarawak in 1841. But before we proceed to a survey of Sarawak, let us take note of the political partition of the island of Borneo as it existed on the eve of the creation of Malaysia in 1963.

Sarawak had an area of 48,250 square miles, and Sabah (North Borneo) of 29,388 square miles. The area of the British protected State of Brunei was 2,226 square miles. The population of Brunei in 1960 was 83,877 (estimated at 86,500 in 1962). Thus 'British Borneo' had a total area of about 80,000 square miles with a population of about 1,283,000. As against this, the area of Indonesian Borneo, or Kalimantan as it is now called, was about 207,000 square miles, with an estimated population of 4 million.

SARAWAK

At the census of June 1960, the population of Sarawak totalled 744,529.

An estimate for June 1962 gave it as 776,990, made up as follows:[12]

CULTURAL GROUP	POPULATION	PERCENTAGE OF TOTAL
Chinese	244,435	31·5
Sea Dayak	241,544	31·1
Malay	136,232	17·5
Land Dayak	60,890	7·8
Melanau	45,976	5·9
Other Indigenous	39,262	5·1
Other Non-Indigenous	6,914	0·9
European	1,737	0·2

The Chinese, it will be seen, were the majority community by a short head over the Sea Dayaks. This was a fact of outstanding political and social significance both for Sarawak and Malaysia as a whole and it justifies us in starting with a description of the Chinese community.

First of all, let us consider the various 'tribes', or dialect-groups, which together made up the Chinese of Sarawak.

The largest group was the Hakka (Kheh) especially in the First Division. Originally Hakkas from different parts of Kwangtung Province in China formed separate associations. Thus there was the Pu-i Association for those from Tapu Hsien, and the Kiaying Hakka Association for those from the Kiaying Prefecture. Later a general Hakka Association was set up, though the two smaller Associations continued to exist with diminished responsibilities. The second most numerous group was from Foochow. In the Third Division they were in the majority, and the town of Sibu was known both in China and Sarawak as the 'New Foochow'. In Sibu, Foochow speakers were to be found in every occupation; in Kuching and the First Division they were mostly engaged in the building trade, but were to be found also as barbers and coffee-shop keepers.

The Henghua group hailed originally from the Sienya District in Fukien. Most of those of this group in Sarawak came from only two districts and bore the same half dozen or so surnames. They were also to be found in Sandakan and Tawau in North Borneo, and in Malacca. In Kuching 96 per cent of the fishermen were of this group. The Fukien group actually came from the southern part of Fukien where the Amoy dialect is spoken. Traditionally, Hokkiens (as they are generally called) were identified with the export trade, but they had in recent times penetrated into almost every trade and occupation. Next to the Teochius they were the second most numerous group in the grocery business and they dominated the miscellaneous goods stores. They were also strong in the goldsmiths' business and as money-agents remitting money to China. The Chanan (Chao An) group was included by the census authorities with the Hokkiens, but though this classification might be linguistically justified, they still retained their individuality. The Teochiu (Teochew or Chaochow) group (whose dialect was spoken in the eastern part of Kwangtung (Swatow, etc.)) form the most numerous Chinese community in Thailand. Teochius dominated the grocery trade. The Cantonese group represented those who originated from Canton and surrounding districts, near Macao, and from Hong Kong. There was also the Luichow group from the Luichow Peninsula, and the Hainan (Hailam) group from the island of that name. The latter group was outstandingly associated with the coffee-shop business in Sarawak and also with the occupation of cooks and seamen in European and Chinese employment.

It must not be supposed, however, that all Sarawak Chinese were urban. The Hakkas, for example, were mainly farmers in China and in Sarawak their economic role was the same. Nearly all the labour on the rubber-estates in the First Division was Hakka. In fact there was a cleavage within the Chinese community arising from difference in economic function, as well as one between the Chinese and the indigenous peoples.

The criticisms made against the Sarawak Chinese were similar to those made against their fellows in other countries of Southeast Asia, namely that they looked to China rather than their country of adoption as the object of their loyalties; that they were 'capitalistic' and had accumulated for themselves an unfair share of the wealth of the country; that they remitted money to China for the support of their relatives, at the expense of Sarawak; that they were able to educate their children better than could the indigenous peoples; and others of the same sort. The major charge, however, was that they were 'unassimilable'. The truth, in Sarawak, as elsewhere in the region, is that the character of the Chinese community was the product of local circumstances. Given equal citizenship rights and equal opportunities to associate themselves with the country they lived in, the Chinese would identify themselves more and more with it as a 'nation'. Now that immigration had practically been stopped, this was more likely to happen than hitherto.

The largest and most important of the indigenous people was the Sea Dayak group, largely pagan, and farming people mostly, centred in the Second and Third Divisions. The name Sea Dayak is a misnomer due to some ancient misunderstanding, for they are an *inland* people – many think of themselves as Ibans and others object to the term Sea Dayak. They were a comparatively homogenous community and possessed a distinguishable culture. In their language there were strong local variations but it was nevertheless distinctive and mutually intelligible among the sub-groups and well recognized as a native language of Sarawak. Many schools in the Sea Dayak area conducted their lower classes through its medium. They were a healthy and virile race, above the normal intelligence, and had maintained their position as a percentage of the indigenous population over the years (46 per cent, 1947: 47 per cent, 1960).

Next in number came the Malays. They lived in towns and along the coast where they had been a powerful influence for centuries – so powerful that they had always drawn new blood from the pagan tribes. Thus there had arisen a confusion between the Melanaus and the Malays. The intermarriage of a Melanau and a Malay generally meant the conversion of the Melanau to Islam and the children would be regarded as Malay.

Migration had not been an important factor in the growth of the Malay community since 1947. The Malay stronghold was the

Kuching administrative district where more than one-third of their group lived. After Kuching they were most numerous in Sadong and Saribas.

After the Malays, in order of numbers, came the Land Dayaks. Their increase was the greatest recorded for any indigenous community – 36,963 in 1939, 42,195 in 1947, 60,890 in 1960. There is reason to doubt the accuracy of the 1939 count but their increase was undoubted. It was not due to their virility, for Mr Noakes, the superintendent of the 1947 census, remarked 'Observers with a substantial knowledge of these people generally agree that they live under unhygienic conditions and as a group they appear to be of a physically low standard. It is generally agreed that the best efforts of past administration have not been directed towards them.' The Land Dayaks lived in four districts of the First Division – Serian, Kuching, Kural, Bau, and Lundu.

The Melanaus, between whom and the Malays there had been confusion in the minds of the census officials, were a Third and Fourth Division Community: pagans, coastal dwellers, and sago workers.

Other indigenous communities enumerated in the 1960 census were the Bisaya, Kedayan, Kayan, Kenyah, Kelabit, Murut and Punan.

How was this diverse community to be welded into a 'nation'? The answer turned on education. *Sarawak: Report for the year 1962* (HMSO 1963), p. 147 states:

Two principal objectives in Government educational policy have been to narrow the gap in educational standards between the Native peoples and the Chinese, and to bring the different school systems which have grown up in the past into a common national system. The year 1962 saw good progress towards the attainment of both these aims.

In 1946 the gap between the native peoples and the Chinese had been very wide. There were then two well developed school systems available to the Chinese. One was a system of primary and secondary schools which used Chinese (Mandarin) as the medium of instruction and were under the management of committees elected by local

Chinese communities. The other system consisted of English-medium schools managed by Christian missions. For the native peoples there was very little indeed; Government provided for the Malays a number of vernacular primary schools which did not prepare their pupils for any form of secondary education. For the Dayaks and other indigenous peoples there were a few schools provided by Christian missions. As a consequence of this unequal provision, the native people were able to play little part in the civil service and none in the professions. The 1947 census revealed that 98 per cent of the largest native group, the Sea Dayaks, were illiterate. Out of a total indigenous population of 395,417, there was not a single graduate, and only one person (a Malay) had obtained the Cambridge School Certificate.

Since 1946, however, the preoccupation of the Education Department had been to train native teachers and to build up a system of primary schools to serve the Dayaks and Malays under the management of a local authority. By 1962 the situation had radically improved. It was then possible to require native candidates for the training college to have received at least three years of secondary education. By the end of 1961, there had been established 600 native primary schools, and during 1962 seventy more were opened. In addition there were 112 primary schools in native areas managed by the church and missions. In native schools, English was the medium of instruction, though many of the schools made use of Malay, Dayak, etc., in the primary classes.

History

Up to the Japanese occupation of 1942, the history of Sarawak is that of the Brooke family.

The founder of the dynasty, James Brooke (1803–68), entered the East Indian Army in 1819. After being seriously wounded in the First Burma War he quitted the Service in 1830. Inheriting £30,000 on his father's death, Brooke fitted out a yacht, carefully trained its crew, and in October 1838 sailed for Sarawak. He arrived at an opportune time, for a revolt was in progress against the Sultan of Brunei, and Brooke took the leading part in suppressing it. For this he was rewarded with the title of Raja of Sarawak, and was given this province to administer. This appointment was officially effected on 24 September 1841.

Brooke's first concern was to introduce just and humane administration into a country which had been notoriously misgoverned (or not governed at all) and to suppress piracy, but simultaneously he was trying to interest the British Government in Brunei. With the growth of steamship traffic to China, the need had arisen for a coaling station between Singapore and Hong Kong. Brunei itself and the island of Labuan both possessed seams of excellent coal, and Brooke learned that the Dutch were casting covetous eyes on both.

Meanwhile, Brooke's measures against piracy had aroused bitter hostility among the piratical faction of the Sultan of Brunei's nobles who saw their profits threatened, and they attempted to procure Brooke's murder. The sultan's governors of the Sea Dayaks, whose raids on Sarawak Brooke had defeated, planned a big attack on Brooke in 1843, but were foiled by the timely arrival of Captain Keppel, R.N., in HMS *Dido*. In 1846, Brooke and Admiral Cochrane appeared at the entrance to the river on which the town of Brunei now stands, and when the sultan refused to negotiate regarding his support for the pirates, a sharp fight ensued and the sultan fled the island. On agreeing to co-operate with the British in the suppression of piracy he was allowed to return. He now ceded the island of Labuan to Britain, granted Britain most-favoured-nation treatment, and accepted that there should be no alienation of Brunei territory without British consent. At the same time the sultan ceded Sarawak to Brooke in full sovereignty. Brooke then returned to Britain in triumph. He was knighted and appointed Governor of Labuan as well as Consul-General to Brunei and the independent chiefs of Borneo.

The occasion for the extension of Sarawak territory, to such a degree that its area by the 1860s was many times that of its 'parent' Sultanate, was always the suppression of piracy. 'Piracy' (as recent historians have reminded us), comprises many kinds of action ranging from simple robbery on the high seas to the breaking of a blockade by a neutral in a war, and there can be no doubt that

Brooke used piracy-suppression as a weapon of policy. Nevertheless, he acted in good faith according to his lights and was undoubtedly taking legitimate measures to remove the greatest scourge of Malaysian waters. That 'piracy' was to some extent a by-product of the cutting of traditional trade-routes by the Europeans is irrelevant in criticizing him. He was merely dealing with the situation as he found it. His enemies, however, took the line that the alleged 'pirates' were not pirates at all but peaceful natives whom he had wantonly attacked and slaughtered.

Brooke's principal enemies were British Victorian humanitarians. The attack started in the *Straits Times* in 1849 and was taken up by the London *Daily News*. Ultimately David Hume, the Peace Society, the Aborigines Protection Society, Sydney Herbert, and Gladstone himself were drawn into the hostilities against Brooke, with *The Times*, Lord Palmerston, Lord Grey, Keppel and Munday defending him. In 1854, however, Brooke was completely cleared by a Royal Commission. It transpired that Henry Wise, Brooke's former agent, had employed a needy journalist to concoct a false account of the Batang Maru anti-piracy operation in which Brooke had been engaged.

The agitation, however, had in the meantime weakened Brooke's position and earned him other enemies, including the Dutch who greatly resented his presence in Borneo, and had given the impression that he would not receive official British support in a crisis. On this supposition, the Chinese of Kuching, operating within the machinery of their local secret society, staged a revolt against him. Brooke escaped with his life only by diving into the Kuching Creek and swimming under the Chinese junks. Kuching, the capital of Sarawak, was burnt and many Europeans and natives were butchered before the revolt was suppressed.

James Brooke had long ago exhausted his private fortune in keeping Sarawak going, and towards the end of his life it is certain that his state would have become bankrupt without loans to Brooke by his friend and admirer, the Baroness Burdett-Coutts.

Today Brooke remains a hero to most and perhaps still a villain to some. He was succeeded by his nephew, the Tuan Muda, born

Charles Johnson, who adopted the surname Brooke on his accession and who later became Sir Charles Brooke, G.C.M.G. Charles Brooke was also an outstanding character, but his reputation is over-shadowed by that of the first 'White Raja'.

Brunei became a British protectorate in 1878, having reached a condition even nearer complete anarchy than any of the Malay states in the 1870s.

The later history of Sarawak is mainly economic and social. The Brooke policy was that of benevolent dictatorship. The welfare of the peoples of Sarawak, especially the Dayaks, was its main concern. In view of this, Sarawak was not opened to foreign enterprise, and only one company (the Borneo Company) enjoyed any privileges, and those were of a limited nature. So far as possible the indigenous peoples were kept from any interference, and although the Brookes themselves were orthodox Anglicans, no missionary enterprise was permitted in the interior (though this rule was abrogated when Sarawak became a colony). Produce such as sago and pepper was exported, and some gold was mined, and with the advent of rubber this was grown to a limited extent. The great obstacle to the exploitation of the minerals, such as coal, was the prohibition of immigration on any scale. Miri was a rich source of oil until its wells began to be exhausted (in neighbouring Brunei vast oil deposits were discovered in the hills).

On 14 September 1941, three months before the outbreak of the Pacific War, a new constitution was adopted for Sarawak by which the former Supreme Council became the Raja's executive council, and the sole power to legislate was vested in the Raja, acting with the advice and consent of the Council Negri. The Council Negri comprised 25 members, 14 being officially appointed and 11 unofficial representatives of the people, including members of the Chinese community and the native tribes.

On 16 December 1941, Japanese forces landed at Miri and Lutong, and on 28 December the enemy was in possession of the capital. On 21 June 1944 Australian troops landed at Lutong unopposed.

After the liberation in 1945, the last Raja, Sir Charles Vyner

Brooke, agreed with the British Government that the times called for a change in régime. The change, however, was opposed by Anthony Brooke, the son of the Tuan Muda (heir apparent). Nevertheless, on 17 May 1946, the Council Negri, by 19 votes to 16, authorized the Act of Cession to the British Crown and Sarawak became a Crown Colony.

The progress made by Sarawak towards representative govern/ ment before its federation in Malaysia is described later.

SABAH (NORTH BORNEO)

The population of North Borneo (Sabah) at the census held on 10 August 1960 totalled 454,421, composed as follows.[13]

COMMUNITY	POPULATION	PERCENTAGE OF TOTAL
Dusun	145,229	32·0
Murut	22,138	4·9
Bajau	59,710	13·1
Other Indigenous	79,421	17·5
Chinese	104,542	23·0
European	1,896	0·4
Others	41,485	9·1

The Dusuns were the largest racial group, constituting almost one third of the total population. It would seem that they wandered into Borneo from the north, possibly at a time before the last Ice Age ended, when Borneo was still joined to the Philippines. Actually they are a group of sub/tribes, each speaking a dialect which is more or less intelligible to the others. They inhabited chiefly the West Coast and the plains of Tambun and Ranau in the interior. They were rice/growers, 'prosperous and stable'. The Bajaus, a Muslim people, were to be found on both the East and West coasts. They, together with the Ilanuns, Sulus, Obians, Binadans, and kindred tribes, are descendants of the notorious pirates who were the terror of the Malaysian waters until well into the nineteenth century when Raja James Brooke, in association with the British Navy, broke their grip on the sea routes. They had thereafter been diverted from piracy to peaceful pursuits – fishing, rice-planting, and cattle-farming, the last being probably their most important contribution to the country's economy. Of the other indigenous communities the most important were the Bruneis and the Kedayans, both Muslim peoples originating from Malaya, Java, and Sumatra. Their total number was about 25,000, and they are included under the heading of Malays in the summary of the population of Malaysia (page 186). In general they were rice-planters, seamen, and fishermen, and inhabited the West Coast fringe from Brunei Bay to Jesselton.

Of these communities the Muruts were the most primitive. They were not, however, negritos, who are not found in Borneo. They still lived mostly in the past, especially those in the more inaccessible parts of the interior. They had not yet adopted a system of settled agriculture but followed the age-long practice of shifting cultivation, using usually a seven-year cycle by which they were able to obtain a supply of hill rice and tapioca which was enough for them to live on. They were great hunters, using spears, blowpipes with poisoned darts, and dogs. They collected jungle produce for sale, and like the 'Sakais' of Malaya they worked (when they felt like it) on the rubber-estates and small-holdings along the roads and railways from Keningau to Papar. From 1921 (and possibly earlier) their numbers were decreasing, but between 1951 and 1960 had increased by 18 per cent due largely to the fall in mortality consequent on improved hygiene.

Again, as in Sarawak, the Chinese were the largest immigrant community. Their function in Sabah was similar to that which they performed in the other countries of Malaysia. They were engaged in agriculture and commerce, and they supplied most of the artisans for industry and a large proportion of the clerks employed in the civil service and commerce. The business and shop-keeping communities, particularly on the East Coast, were mostly Cantonese who had long established connections with Hong Kong, while in the West Coast towns many were Hokkiens who tended to look towards Singapore.

Among the 'others' (natives of Indonesia, the Philippines, India and Ceylon, Sarawak, the Cocos Islands, Singapore, Malaya), the Indonesians were the most numerous (about 25,000). They were Muslims and racially and culturally similar to the Peninsular Malays but they had not been assimilated into the Malay community, and their national loyalties would have important significance in the hostilities between Indonesia and Malaya over the Federation of Malaysia.

As elsewhere in Malaysia, in Sabah the problem of amalgamating the communities into a nation turned on education. The gulf between the Chinese and the native peoples was, as in Sarawak, an obstacle to its solution. But great progress had been made since the liberation from the Japanese. The literacy rates per thousand had risen from 160 in 1951 to 243 in 1961.

History

The history of the British North Borneo Company begins in a remarkable way for the person who took the first step that led to its creation was not British but American.

The first White Raja of Sarawak, Sir James Brooke, had had his eye on these northern territories as a kind of playground for his pets, the Dayaks. Indeed (as we have already seen), he had secured for Britain what is today part of Sabah, namely the island of Labuan (1846), partly to tap the trade of the northern islands and partly to make safe the China seas. 'British China-bound ships, after passing the three well-lit bazaars of Penang, Malacca, and Singapore, in the dark thieves-alley of the Malacca Straits faced a lonely and perilous path across the China Sea to Canton.'[14] Labuan and Hong Kong lessened the dangers. But the plans of the Brooke family to bring the whole of the north of Borneo under their wing were challenged in 1865 when Claude Lee Moses, the American Consul to Brunei, came upon the scene.

Lee Moses was an adventurer pure and simple, a discarded member of the lower deck of the United States Navy. Being hard up on his arrival at Labuan (he had had to borrow his fare from Singapore) he managed to secure within a few days of his arrival, on the promise of certain payments to the Sultan of Brunei and the heir to the throne, the cession for ten years of a large tract of Brunei territory to the north. Armed with those cession papers he im, mediately left for Hong Kong to see what he could realize on them. Here he sold them to two American merchants, Joseph W. Torrey and Thomas B. Harris, and a Chinese partner of theirs, Wo Hang. The latter soon withdrew and was replaced by two other Chinese. The four thereupon formed 'The American Trading Company of Borneo', with $7,000 capital. Moses undertook to extend the protection of the United States to any Borneo settlement of the Com, pany in return for a third of the profits. Labourers were recruited, a dozen or so Americans were interested in the scheme, and in November 1865, the party sailed. On arrival in Borneo, Torrey was appointed Supreme Ruler and Governor and was given the titles of Raja of Ambong and Marudu and Maharaja of North Borneo by the Sultan of Brunei who vested him with the powers of life and death over the inhabitants, the right to coin money and make laws, and other powers and rights exercised by a sovereign ruler. Sailing north from Brunei, the little expedition settled at the mouth of the Kimamis River, some sixty miles away.

The Kimamis Settlement, however, was a failure. Even if the will to exploit the cessions had been there, the necessary capital was not forthcoming. Lee Moses reverted to penury and the sultan received nothing. But with the changing political scene and the newly awakened desires among the nations of Western Europe for colonies, the cession of the north Bornean lands had become a saleable asset – providing, that is, that the ten,year limit could be extended. In Hong Kong, Torrey secured a partner in the person of Baron von Overbeck, the Austrian Consul,General, another adventurer with a colourful past. A German emigrant to America, he had served on a whaler in the Bering Sea, and then had become a business man in Hong Kong. Here he had been of service to the Austrian Govern, ment in several ways and had been rewarded with a barony and a consulate in return. Overbeck now became the leader and driving force in an effort to obtain financial support on the London money, market for the schemes of himself and his associates to get the Borneo concessions renewed and to sell them to the highest bidder.

His principal partner in these activities was an Englishman named Edward Dent.

But these plans could have had no constructive outcome had it not been that they aroused the interest of a young and enthusiastic member of the Civil Service in Malaya, W. H. Treacher, who was to become the first Governor of North Borneo and then to succeed Swettenham as the Resident-General of the Federated Malay States. Treacher's motive was to bring what he regarded as the wild law-lessness of these territories under civilized administration. He encouraged Overbeck and his associates to proceed to Brunei, to obtain the confirmation of the cession, and to form a company to develop the resources. But the company, he insisted, must be *British*. Overbeck and Dent then went to Brunei, interviewed the sultan, and with a liberal advance of money were able to win him over. On 29 December 1877 the documents were signed in which the sultan made three grants of territory from Gaya Bay on the west coast to the Sibuco River on the east; and the heir apparent, in a grant of his west coast possessions (the rivers Kimamis and Benomi) ceded some 28,000 square miles of territory, embracing some 900 miles of North Bornean coastline, for a total yearly payment of $15,000. But (as the sultan well knew) the territories in question had long ceased to be under Brunei control, were yielding no revenue, and the sultan was to receive $15,000 a year for nothing. Later on, discovering that the Sultan of Sulu claimed the same territory, the British Company obtained another cession from him.

Treacher's intervention had now made it impossible for the ceded territories to be controlled by anything but a British company, and a British company the concessionaries decided to form. For this company, Dent (now in London) determined to obtain a Royal Charter. The move was opposed both by the Foreign and Colonial Offices, and the story of how the charter was eventually obtained forms a fascinating chapter in diplomatic history.[15]

All that need be recorded here is that the Charter was eventually granted – and by the 'anti-imperialist' Prime Minister, Gladstone! By an Order In Council of 1881 the British North Borneo Company came into being.

In the histories of Malaya and other countries the romantic and exciting episodes all relate to the periods of confusion and lawlessness. Once the wild territories are brought under settled administration the record becomes more respectable – and duller. So was it the case with North Borneo.

The original cessions of large tracts of North Borneo to a shadowy British company aroused the protests of Spain, Holland, and the United States, but these protests came to nothing. They were forgotten until the moment that Malaysia was about to be created in 1963, and then they were renewed, vociferously by the Philippines, as the heir of Spain, and by Indonesia (even more vociferously and dangerously) as the heir of Holland. At the time the hostility of the second 'White Raja' of Sarawak, Sir Charles Brooke, was much more serious, but he consoled himself by obtaining what he could of the remainder of the territories of the Sultan of Brunei for his own State of Sarawak. The infant State of North Borneo also began to expand. Treacher, in 1883, at the suggestion of the Admiralty, quickly annexed the uninhabited island of Balambangan and other acquisitions by purchase followed. A vain attempt by Brooke to check the southward march of North Borneo occurred in 1885 when Treacher purchased the small Kawang River territory from its absentee landlord.

The subsequent history of North Borneo up to 1941 falls mainly under the peaceful headings of administration, economic development, labour, health, and education.

Under the first of these headings, however, North Borneo underwent many vicissitudes. These arose to begin with from financial difficulties and by unwise direction of the Chartered Company in London. The finances of the Company were by no means sound and there was a prospect at one time that Raja Charles Brooke would buy the Company's assets. The young state needed gentle nurturing, but D. C. Cowie, the Director who had most influence with the Court, induced his fellow Directors in the early 1890s to abandon their cautious policy of waiting on the development of the territory and to embark on a policy of rash and ill-conceived expenditure. This included the installation of a telegraph line from

Labuan to Sandakan at what turned out to be a great cost to a poor country like Sabah (it was not until 1897 that communication with London was established, by which time the capital cost amounted to £20,000). It cost £4000 a year to maintain and its revenue was only £250. Another project that was to prove even more costly was railway-building – which, however, was to prove of ultimate advantage to the country. The building of this railway was grossly mismanaged, and a clash which took place in 1900 over the control of its construction between Cowie and the Governor of North Borneo, Hugh Clifford of the Malayan Civil Service, led to the latter's resignation after only six months of office.

The fortunes of the territory were not correctly reflected in the dividends paid by the Chartered Company. Apart from a 2½ per cent dividend in 1890 (from the profits of tobacco land sales) no dividend was paid until 1899 when it was 2 per cent. This rate was maintained annually until 1905 when it became 3 per cent; in 1907 it was 4 per cent, and between 1909 and 1914, five per cent. But although the Company entered on a period of ten lean years beginning with the 1914–18 war, it still continued to pay dividends and in order to pay them continued borrowing. By 1924 it was in debt to the incredible amount of £1,649,800. So while North Borneo was being developed on borrowed capital, the Company itself was on the verge of bankruptcy. If it were to escape this fate, a policy of retrenchment must forthwith be adopted, and this was embarked upon by its new President, Sir Neill Malcolm. Although he visited North Borneo several times, he rarely interfered in the administration: his function was mainly financial.

Meanwhile a succession of able Governors were seconded to North Borneo from Malaya, but their handicap was for long the lack of an efficient Civil Service to carry out the administration. This lack was remedied from 1925 onwards when the Company obtained a supply of cadets recommended by the Appointments Boards of the Universities of Oxford and Cambridge. The whole territory was administered by 50–60 of the officers thus recruited.

As regards the economy of Sabah, the company was maintained in the beginning by the export of edible birds' nests, a delicacy much favoured by the Chinese, and this remained a dependable source of revenue throughout the Chartered Company's régime. Jungle produce (rattans, guttapercha, damar gum) later added its tribute. Timber, however, became a much more important industry and was exported in ever-increasing amounts. The cultivation of tobacco also had its prosperous periods, but it was rubber that was to become the staple product. By 1907 there were 3,226 acres planted with rubber with an export of 5,474,560 lbs. But as in Malaya, the industry suffered greatly in the slumps of 1920-1 and of 1930-2.

From the beginning of the Company's rule, Sabah was under-populated and had a crying need for labour. In 1892 Dr José Rizal, the great martyr of Philippine Nationalism, had planned to settle in North Borneo with his followers to get away from Spanish rule, but this came to nothing in the end. China was the obvious source for recruitment, but although many schemes for allocating the influx of Chinese labourers were set on foot, none of them was outstandingly successful. Japanese were also brought in small numbers. In 1934, the Archbishop of Canterbury proposed to find shelter in North Borneo for Assyrian refugees from Iraq. The Chartered Company offered them shelter, but the Archbishop was deterred by the cost of transporting the refugees to their new home (they finally found shelter in British Guiana). As the chairman of the North Borneo Planters' Association said in 1940, 'the present labour position is bad and is getting worse.' After the liberation in 1945, the labour situation was worse than ever, for political events had resulted in a complete drying up of the one important reservoir of supply – China.

While efforts were being made to solve the problems of revenue and economy, steps were taken to secure the indigenous peoples in the possession of their land. The task of issuing land-titles was made extremely difficult by the various native rights. With secure title-deeds, the Dusuns, Bajaus, and Basayas proved to be more efficient agriculturalists. But an abuse which resisted elimination was the indebtedness of the native herdsmen to the Chinese traders. Piracy had been effectively suppressed, but when the Chartered Company assumed control, slavery was still common. Such was the energy with which it was then attacked that by 1903 it had, by and large, vanished from North Borneo. The record of the Chartered Company in native administration was a notably good one.

From 10 January 1942 until 10 September 1945, Sabah was occupied by the Japanese. During the occupation the country suffered greatly, on the one hand from the stresses and shortages caused by the war and from the action of the invaders, and on the other from the actual hostilities, especially from Allied bombing in the later stages, resulting in the complete destruction of the principal towns. The task of the British when they returned was mainly one of rehabilitation and reconstruction. This was to occupy many years to come.

After the liberation, it was decided that, in return for compensation, the Chartered Company should transfer its sovereign rights to the Crown. This took place on 26 June 1946, on which date British North Borneo became a Crown Colony. Its name was changed to North Borneo. Under the agreement the sum to be paid in respect of sovereign rights and assets was to be settled by arbitration. A sum of £860,000 on account, out of which the Company was to redeem debentures, was paid at the end of the year.

The beginnings of representative government in Sabah are discussed in chapter 8, but it is clear that it had not progressed very far before Sabah became part of Malaysia in 1963.

83 Sir James Brooke, created Raja of Sarawak by the Sultan of Brunei in 1841 for helping to suppress a revolt, was the founder of the dynasty that provided benevolent dictatorship in Sarawak until 1942. Portrait by Francis Grant.

84 The suppression of piracy and the presence of coal essential to the steamship traffic to China led Sir James Brooke to make war in 1846 on the Sultan of Brunei who secretly supported the pirates. As a result the island of Labuan was ceded to Britain and Sarawak to Brooke himself in full sovereignty.

85 Hoisting the British flag on Labuan.

86 Audiences with the Sultan of Brunei took place in his Council Chamber, a somewhat fanciful contemporary version of which is shown here.

87–88 'Piracy' remained the excuse for the extension of the territory of Sarawak for many years. These engravings of a pirate and of pirate ships are from a contemporary Portuguese account and from Brooke's own story of his adventures.

89 The Chinese came to trade and settle many centuries before the British, and now constitute the largest cultural group in Sarawak and Sabah.

90 The Brookes did not open Sarawak to further immigration or foreign enterprise. The Borneo Company alone enjoyed limited privileges, including gold mining.

91 The Land Dayaks are one of the largest of the minority cultural groups of Sarawak. Like the Ibans, mis-named Sea Dayaks, they live inland in rows of dwelling units on stilts, a number of which joined together constitute long-houses such as these.

92 In his part of a long-house, the paramount chief of the Sea Dayaks sits with a Sea Dayak boy from one of the British schools.

93 Selling fish at Brunei town.

94 The addition of Western industry to the more traditional economy of natural produce has its cultural by-products. Vegetables on sale at Kuala Belait.

95 Lutong oil refinery, Sarawak.

96 Sago logs ready for rasping. Sago has long been an important export from Sarawak.

97   In spite of the strongest opposition from President Sukarno of Indonesia, the Federation of Malaysia comprising Malaya, Singapore, Sarawak and Sabah was proclaimed on 15 September 1963, conferring independence on the latter three at the same time. The City Hall of Singapore was the scene of this Malaysia day ceremony.

98   Voting by thumb-print in Jesselton, the capital of Sabah, November 1962, the result of which sanctioned incorporation into Malaysia.

8   Malaysia

IT IS TRUE TO SAY that whereas the Chinese of Singapore in general desired amalgamation with the Federation, the Malays of the Federation in general (in so far, of course, as they were politically-minded) were opposed to it, and, indeed, to any close association with the (then) Colony. The reasons for this were plain. In the Federation, the Malays were still in a sizeable majority numerically over the Chinese, and the possession of automatic citizenship gave them a further advantage electorally over them, but should Singapore be amalgamated with the Federation, this advantage would be at once lost. The franchise in Singapore was universal for all adults, male and female, and the addition of some half a million fully enfranchised Chinese voters to the rolls might mean that the Malays would be outvoted at the elections – especially, if there were any considerable Chinese immigration from Singapore.

But as the political situation developed, the views of the Federation Malays, and of Tunku Abdul Rahman in particular, underwent a change. It was almost certainly the renewed activity among the Chinese Communists, especially in Singapore, which was responsible for this. Should the Communists be successful in taking over in Singapore, Singapore being self-governing and perhaps fully independent by this time, it could prove to be a poisonous thorn in the side of the Federation Government. And since the Singapore Chinese generally desired union with the Federation, it might be possible to devise a form of association which would stop short of an amalgamation and thus safeguard the position of the Malays in the Federation. However, if this new association, or federation, were to be confined to the Federation of Malaya and Singapore, the Chinese, representing some 3·8 million in a total population of 8·5 million, as compared with some 3·7 million 'Malaysians', would be in a slight majority and it would be difficult to keep the political balance. But if the neighbouring British territories in Borneo, Sarawak, North Borneo (Sabah), and Brunei, themselves on the way towards independence, were included this would form a federation in which the Chinese represented some 4·2 million in a total population of some 9·8 million (including the non-Malay races). Was this solution at all feasible?

The following table showing the population of the Federation of Malaysia before the secession of Singapore draws attention to facts of great political and social significance.

POPULATION OF MALAYSIA (IN THOUSANDS) IN 1960
AND RACIAL BREAK-DOWN

	Malays	Chinese	Indians & Pakistanis	Borneo Indigenous (Non-Malay)	Others	Total
FEDERATION OF MALAYA	3,461a	2,552	773	—	123	6,909
SINGAPORE	227a	1,231	138	—	38	1,634
SARAWAK	129	229	2	378	6	744
NORTH BORNEO	25	105	3	283	39b	455
TOTAL	3,842	4,117	916	661	206	9,742c

a. Includes persons of Indonesian origin who have been largely absorbed into the Malay Community[16]
b. Includes 25,000 Indonesians
c. The total population in 1964 was about 10·5 million

Tunku Abdul Rahman came to the conclusion that it was. It is to his speech of 27 May 1961 at a Singapore Press Luncheon, that the initiation of the 'Greater Malaysia' proposals can be traced. Among other points he made in the speech were these:

. . . The Singapore Government has also been doing all they can for the people, but the Prime Minister of Singapore has quite a different type of people to deal with. In Singapore, where the Chinese predominate, the natural tendency is to try to make the State a 'little China'. While in Malaya the Government is characteristically Malayan and bases its policy on a Malayan way of life and Malayan standards. This is exactly what the Singapore Prime Minister wants to do too. . . .

Malaya today as a nation realises that she cannot stand alone and in isolation. Outside of international politics, the national one must be broad-based. Sooner or later she should have an understanding with Britain and the peoples of the territories of Singapore, North Borneo, Brunei, and Sarawak.

It is premature for me to say now how this closer understanding can be brought about, but it is inevitable that we should look ahead to this objective and think of a plan whereby those territories can be brought closer together in political and economic co-operation.

This apparently revolutionary proposal by the Prime Minister of the Federation, not only for a 'merger' with Singapore but with territories outside Malaya, might on the face of things have been expected to produce a united protest from all parties opposed to the Alliance Party. But the significant fact was that among all parties, including those of the Singapore 'Left', there was no opposition to the *idea* of a merger between Singapore and the Federation, only a complete difference of opinion as to the *terms* of such a merger. PAP had indeed included a merger with the Federation as one of its election pledges. Barisan Socialis, the new Socialist Front opposing the PAP Government, declared that they sought 'a genuine reunification of our country and peoples' with the entry of Singapore as a 'state' on the same basis as the other states, and 'with all its citizens automatically becoming citizens of the Federation, and having all the rights, privileges, and obligations, like any of the other citizens of the Federation'. But this, of course, would have amounted to the amalgamation which UMNO was determined to avoid. Mr Lee Kuan-Yew, on the other hand (as we shall see in a moment), realizing that the Malays could scarcely be expected to yield at one move their 'special position' in the Federation of Malaya, was prepared to support a federal association of a less complete kind. At the same time he sought to retain certain reserved privileges for the State of Singapore inside any federation. What was new in Tunku Abdul Rahman's suggestion, however, was the inclusion of the Borneo territories in the proposed 'Malaysia'.

In September 1961, the two Prime Ministers met in Kuala Lumpur to discuss the question. On his return to Singapore Mr Lee Kuan Yew said that the talks had been very successful and that a Joint Working Party had been appointed to work out the details. The main problems had already been ironed out, he said, and Singapore would be 'a very special State' with certain subjects (finance, labour, and education) reserved to it.

Having come to a general agreement between themselves, the two Prime Ministers had now to carry their respective legislatures with them on the matter. The next step would be to approach the British Government, who would have the final say since Britain still retained responsibility for the Borneo territories; Sarawak and North Borneo were Colonies and Brunei was a protectorate; and Singapore also, though self-governing, was still a Colony.

A month or two after this meeting, in the House of Representatives in Kuala Lumpur, Tunku Abdul Rahman won a victory for his 'Malaysia' plans when after a three-day debate a motion was approved giving him the necessary mandate for talks in London with the Prime Minister Mr Macmillan for transfer of sovereignty over the state of Singapore and the Borneo territories to a new Malaysia Federation. His speech stressed that Malaya was linked to the Borneo territories not only by proximity and close association but also because the latter had the same types of culture and racial origins as the Malayans. Their territories, however, like the Federation, had a diversity of races. The two territories had similar customs, similar problems, shared the same currency, and their civil services had grown up in the same [British] tradition and on the same principles of service. Yet the slowness of their constitutional development was in marked contrast to the swift developments in other British colonies in Africa or Asia. It was the duty of the Federation to help them bring about an end to any form of colonialism.

The next step was to obtain agreement to the proposals on the part of the British Government. To this end Tunku Abdul Rahman went to London in November 1961 and, in consequence, an agreement was signed between the United Kingdom and the Federation preparing the way for the creation of a Federation of Malaysia. The question of the retention of the military bases was left open, for it was clear that the Federation of Malaysia itself would have to come to a decision on this point when it came into being. It could not be pre-committed to a decision. So far as the Tunku himself was concerned, however, he had no objection to the British retaining their military bases.

Meanwhile, Mr Lee Kuan Yew was faced with the somewhat more difficult task of swaying Singapore opinion in favour of the merger. This task he applied himself to with his customary energy, and among the means he adopted to this end was to give a series of twelve talks on the subject over Radio Malaya.

Mr Lee told his Singapore audience that soon they would have to decide on their own future. In a few months the constitutional arrangements for the merger would be settled. In this series of broadcasts he hoped to tell them what this merger meant, why it was good for all of them, and why some people were deliberately creating trouble and difficulty over it to prevent it from taking place.

Everyone knew (the Prime Minister said) that this merger was inevitable. The Tunku and PAP were agreed on the matter, and even the Communists said that the merger must take place. The artificial barrier of the Johore Causeway was in fact only a temporary one and it was only a matter of time before it was swept aside. The merger was 'as inevitable as the rising and setting of the sun'. If it did not come by the consent of the peoples of the two territories, then inevitably it would come by the use of force by one territory over the other, because each was vital to the survival of the other.

The reason that the Federation was important to Singapore (Mr Lee went on) was because it was the hinterland which produced the rubber and tin that 'keep our shop-window economy going'. Without this economic base Singapore could not survive. Without the reunification of their two governments and an integration of their two economies both their economic positions would slowly and steadily get worse. Singapore would suffer more than the Federation because it had fewer resources to fall back on. Merger would mean that they would have one integrated economy and that the wasteful duplication of facilities in the two territories would come to an end. They had an international rubber market in Singapore. The Federation was on the point of setting up its own rubber market to compete with Singapore and take away Singapore's business. With a Singapore separated from the Federation they would be cutting each other's throats.

Singapore on the other hand, Mr Lee continued, considered it essential that they should have local autonomy in education and labour policies. But these seemingly non-controversial propositions had aroused a great deal of noisy protest from interested quarters. The most important interested party was the Malayan Communist Party (MCP). This was an illegal organization. Since the Communists were unable to make official statements in the press or through other channels of information they had to work through proxies, they had sympathizers and secret party members in the lawful political parties, in the unions, cultural organizations, and old boys' associations who 'made appropriate noises on their behalf'. Of course they had not been so foolish as to oppose merger openly. They had all agreed on merger in principle. But they wanted a different kind of merger, one in which security was not under the control of the central government. They were, through their agencies, trying to cloud and confuse the merger issue so that the people of Singapore would come to the wrong decision.

For years after the Emergency began in 1948, Communism had been painted in terms of violence, terror, brutality, and evil. There *was* violence, terror and brutality, and there *were* evil men in the Communist Party. But this was not the whole story, for if it were as simple as that the Communists would have perished with the collapse of their own armed revolt. The fact was that with all their weaknesses they had some strong qualities which had permitted their survival. Although they had no chance in the foreseeable future of capturing power by force of arms, they had been able to continue the struggle for the Communist cause through new methods. Many of their old supporters in the jungle had died or been banished but some had drifted back anonymously into the towns. Only a hard core remained on the Malayan–Thai border. But new recruits had been found among the idealistic young men and women, largely from Chinese middle schools in Malaya, both in the Federation and Singapore. These were the new men and women fighting under different conditions with different methods and tactics to create a Communist Malaya.

Mr Lee Kuan Yew then went on to describe the way the Communists went to work, drawing on his personal experience of them and their leaders. At the time of the middle school riots of 1959 he and his colleagues had come into contact with the Chinese educated world – a world teeming with vitality, dynamism and revolution, a world in which the Communists had been working for the last few years with considerable success. 'We the English educated revolutionaries went in trying to tap this oil field of political resources and soon found our pipelines crossing those of the Communist Party. We were latecomers trying to tap the same oil fields. We were considered by the Communists as poaching on their exclusive territory.' Many of the Communist leaders were not crooks or opportunists (said Mr Lee) – they were merely mistaken in their methods and aims. Mr Lee said that he used to spend hours arguing with them trying to prove that whatever else happened in China or Russia, they and he were living in *Malaya* and, irrespective of Communism or democratic socialism, if they wanted to build a more just and equal society in Malaya, they would have to make some fundamental decisions, such as being *Malayans*, uniting the Chinese and Indians and others with the Malays, building up national unity and national loyalty, and rallying all the races together through a national language. 'We want merger and independence. The Communists do not. They have a vested interest in entering the anti colonial struggle so that under cover of anti colonialism they can advance Communism. They want the anti colonial struggle to go on, meanwhile using Singapore as a base to undermine Malaya.'

The two Prime Ministers were now in alliance for the same end. But this did not by any means entail a complete coincidence of method or aim. The Tunku was a Malay and an uncompromising enemy of Communism, the USSR, and Communist China. Mr Lee was a Malayan Chinese who had tried to work with Chinese Communists in the past and had to rely to a large extent for his political success in converting Chinese who had Communistic leanings to his own point of view. This divergence between the two men was brought out in September 1962, when Mr Lee Kuan Yew paid a visit to Moscow. Questioned on this subject by the press on 20 September, Tunku Abdul Rahman replied:

It came as a surprise to me that he (Mr Lee Kuan Yew) has gone to Moscow. From what I know, he has been attacking the Communists and those parties which he suspects of having connection with Communism. His visit to Moscow will naturally nullify what he has said. Perhaps he has gone there to see for himself how bad the Communists can be. Until I have seen him and hear from him the reason for his visit, it is not possible for me to say whether he was right or wrong in going there. . . .

The next day the Tunku amplified this statement by saying:

Enche Boestamam and other political leaders have expressed surprise that I should be objecting to Mr Lee Kuan Yew's visit to Moscow and it was suggested that I should make a point of going there myself. According to them, I have visited Britain and America and so why not Moscow too. They fail to appreciate the point that if I were to visit Moscow and take advantage of the hospitality of the Russian Government it would not be right for me to refuse to welcome or entertain the Prime Minister and the other leaders of Russia should they express a wish to come here . . . on the other hand, Britain and America are our friends and inasmuch as they made me feel welcome in their countries I would consider myself privileged to welcome their leaders here. Not so with the Communists. Twelve years' atrocities and murders committed in Malaya against the innocent and peaceful citizens of this country can't be easily forgotten. . . . If they were to be encouraged to come here, could we prevent the uprise of the Communist morale in Malaya, and consequently encourage the start of another outbreak of Communist terrorism?

This incident, though it was to have no enduring influence on the relationships between the two Prime Ministers, illustrates the very different situations in which they found themselves.

While the Tunku was armed with the unanimous approval of his legislature for the merger, Mr Lee Kuan-Yew, having lost his overall majority in his legislature, decided to submit the question of a merger to a referendum. This was held on 1 September 1962. Of the 624,000 Singapore citizens automatically registered as electors, 561,559, or 90 per cent, voted under the system of compulsory voting first introduced for the 1959 general election. Of those voting, 397,626, or 71 per cent, voted for Alternative A, the Government's proposals which allowed Malayan citizenship to all Singapore citizens and reserved autonomy on matters of education and labour; 9,422 for Alternative B, of merger like any other state of the Federation; and 7,911 for Alternative C which offered merger on terms no less favourable than those offered to the Borneo territories. There were also 144,077, or 25 per cent, blank votes cast under the inspiration of the joint campaign of the Barisan Socialis, the United People's Party, the Workers' Party, the Liberal Socialist Party, and the United Democratic Party – the first with 16 members out of 51 in the Assembly, and the latter two unrepresented there. The result was a triumph for the PAP Government, and was regarded by Mr Lee as a decisive rejection of Communist propaganda on the part of the people of Singapore.

It was one thing, however, for the Prime Minister of the Federation and Singapore to agree on the proposed federation, and to carry their people with them, but it was another thing to incorporate the British Borneo territories into it. Britain was still the sovereign power in Sarawak, North Borneo, and Brunei, and it was certain that the British Government would not agree to cede sovereignty to a Malaysia Federation including them until their leaders and peoples had been consulted. To this end a commission was appointed jointly by the British and Federation Governments on 16 January 1962, with Lord Cobbold as Chairman, two other British members, and two Federation of Malaya members (one of Malay and the other of Chinese race). The commission was charged with the task of ascertaining the views of the peoples of North Borneo and Sarawak on the proposed merger. At the same time the views of the Sultan of Brunei were being separately sought.

Until 1941 the government of Sarawak was a benevolent despotism, but in that year the Raja began to rule through a constitution – in which experiment the Japanese interrupted him. In 1956 a new constitution was granted with a Council Negri consisting of 24 elected members and 2 standing members appointed for life prior to the Cession. There was a further advance towards democratic government foreshadowed in the White Paper of October 1961 which called for the extension of the franchise to all persons over the age of twenty-one – subject to residential qualifications and the usual disqualifications – and a reconstruction of the Council Negri. According to the White Paper, it was proposed to associate some unofficials of the Supreme Council with the function and presenta-tion of government policy on certain subjects. This would be a stage in the advance towards the ministerial system of government which (the Governor felt) would be a most valuable exercise in responsibility.

We see, then, in Sarawak, a gradual advance towards democracy, conceded and planned by the metropolitan Power, reminding one somewhat of the Montagu-Chelmsford reforms or 'Dyarchy' in India a generation or so before. But the spread of the process was in marked contrast to the swift acceleration towards independence recently manifested in the Federation of Malaya and (at a somewhat lesser speed) in Singapore.

The Cobbold Report began with Sarawak. A most fundamental question in the multi-racial society of Sarawak (it said) was that of race relations. In recent years relations between the different com-munities had been excellent and the country had consequently been a happy one. The indigenous people on the one hand, and the immigrant races, in this case the Chinese, on the other, had been on the whole satisfied to go their separate ways. However, this state of affairs could only last as long as political power remained with the colonial authority. The commission had seen in Sarawak the conflict arising when a transfer of power was contemplated in some form and the indigenous people became aware of the prospect of having to share political power with the immigrant races at a time when they felt themselves still economically backward.

Uneasiness was felt at the time of the first elections when the first political party to come into existence in Sarawak, the Sarawak United People's Party (SUPP) was formed with predominantly Chinese leadership. Taken as a signal for the beginning of the bid for power by the non-natives at a time when the natives felt themselves not yet in a position to compete, this increased the strain in race relations springing from the unbalance in economic power. For this reason the Party Negara (PANAS) and later the Sarawak National Party (SNP), with native leadership, came into being. This was followed by the formation of Barisan Anak Jati Sarawak (BARJASA) with its proposal to enter into an alliance with SNP. The proposals for a Malaysia Federation and the prospect of independence within the Federation had served to accentuate these developments. The alignment of political forces along racial lines, though understandable (said the Cobbold Report) was a matter of the gravest concern.

The position in Sarawak was further exacerbated (the Report continued) by the fact that the present Government in Malaya, which would clearly be an important force in the new Federation of Malaysia, was anti-Communist. In the absence of some project like Malaysia, the Chinese, with their rapidly increasing population and their long start over the other races in education, could expect when independence came, to be in an unassailable position in Sarawak. This, in turn, could put the Communists, with their highly developed organization to work on the fears and frustrations of the great body of non-Communist Chinese, in an equally unassailable position. The Malaysia proposals would interfere with this development. Communist elements had therefore worked ceaselessly to exaggerate the fears which the Chinese community as a whole and members of other communities had of Malay domination and to make capital out of every possible issue, e.g. as to whether there should be a special position for the natives, citizenship, national language, and religion. They had also worked on the emotions of a large body of younger Chinese who had been educated in Chinese schools, who were strongly nationalistic and who had feelings of frustration and anxiety about their prospects. The activities and methods adopted by the extreme left-wing groups, the hard core of which consisted of young Chinese, had antagonized the other communities and indeed many Chinese had drawn the attention of the country as a whole to the possibility of communal friction, which was being deliberately fanned by Communist elements.

The attitude of the indigenous population on the one hand and of the immigrant race on the other to the concept of the Head of State was an interesting reflection on the communal conflict. The constitutional niceties of the concept might not be fully understood by many sections, except the more politically sophisticated, of a population which had been accustomed in the last 120 years to a Head of State, a Raja or a Governor, who wielded executive powers. There was therefore a confusion in the popular mind between the functions of a constitutional Head of State and those of the officer who actually wields executive authority. There was no confusion of mind, however, about the transfer of authority in the new Federation from the British Government to the peoples of the territories, and the Head of State had become a symbol of this transfer of power. The native races therefore had insisted that the Head of State should be a native, reflecting their concept of the return of the power of government from the British Government to themselves, and the immigrant races had for their part insisted that anyone born in Sarawak should be eligible for the office, reflecting their concept of the transfer of power from the British Government to the people of Sarawak. The native population's insistence on a native being the Head of State stemmed in the main from the anxiety to utilize what they believed were the political powers of the office to correct the imbalance of economic power between themselves and the immigrant races.

As regards relations between Malays and the other indigenous people, although there were no ideological overtones here, the Commission found that the prospect of Malaysia was viewed by non-Malay natives in certain parts of the country within the framework of their unhappy recollection of Brunei domination in the past, which was regarded as Malay domination, and of their fear of its return with the new Federation. The suggested name of Malaysia for the new Federation, of Malay for the national language, and of Islam as the national religion, had tended to emphasize these mis-givings.

In the course of collecting their evidence the commission noted the high esteem in which the British colonial administration was held in Sarawak. Generous tributes were paid by all communities to the impartiality of the colonial administrators and to the progress that had been made since the war. The wish was expressed from almost every quarter that the new arrangements should not cause an exodus of the present officials, but should rather encourage them to remain in service in Sarawak until their places could be taken by the local people with the necessary qualifications.

Between Sarawak and North Borneo the commission became conscious of similarities and dissimilarities and of the surprisingly little 'come and go' between the two territories. The conflict of opinion in North Borneo after the Malaysia proposals were put forward followed similar lines to those met with in Sarawak, with the important difference that it had not been bedevilled by the inter-vention of Communist influence. In North Borneo, as in Sarawak, a major stand in the opposition to Malaysia among the Chinese lay in genuine fear of the discrimination which they believed would be practised on them, affecting their education, language, and culture generally, and reducing them to the status of what was popularly known as 'second-class citizens'. Those anxieties were honestly held and should receive serious consideration. There was also fear among the Chinese business community that Malaysia would involve a new and heavier taxation structure.

The Cobbold Commission reported that a third of the people of the two Borneo territories were in favour of Federation; a third would accept if given certain safeguards; while the rest either wanted independence first or would prefer the continuance of British rule.

The commission reached a considerable measure of agreement on the appropriate basis for entry of the Borneo territories into the Federation of Malaysia. There was, however, a fundamental divergence on the question of *phasing*, as to whether the Federation should be formed in one or two stages. The general recommenda¿ tions of the commission included: (*a*) that a decision of principle about the future of the territories should be taken by Governments as soon as possible; (*b*) that the existing Constitution of the Federation of Malaya should be taken as the basis of the new Federation; (*c*) as regards 'Who should be eligible as Head of the Federation', they left the matter open; (*d*) that the name of the Federation should be 'Malaysia'; (*e*) as regards religion, feeling ran high, and there was a difference of opinion between the members of the Commission– the Chairman and British members recommended that there should be complete freedom of religion, education, and propagation of ideas in the Borneo territories, while the Malayan members wanted Islam to be the national religion of the Federation; (*f*) as regards language the Chairman and British members favoured Malay and English as the official languages, but the Malayan members, while insisting that, as in Malaya, Malay should be the official language, were willing that English should continue alongside Malay as an official language for ten years at least; and (*g*) that immigration control must rest with the Central Government of the Federation. The commission also made recommendations regarding citizenship of a detailed and technical nature. They were opposed to the creation of a separate citizenship for the Borneo territories that would carry with it nationality of Malaysia (on the lines of the Malaya–Singapore merger agreement which agreed that a Singapore citizenship should be retained which would automatically carry with it nationality of the new Federation of Malaysia). A provision recommended was that a person resident in Sarawak or North Borneo on the date when Malaysia came into being should be eligible to apply for citizenship of Malaysia if he had resided there for a period of 8 out of the preceding 12 years.

The commission's terms of reference did not cover Brunei, but Tunku Abdul Rahman visited Brunei personally and obtained the unanimous approval of the Sultan in Council to the Malaysia proposals but (as we shall see) hostility among a section of his subjects to the proposed merger was to result in a rebellion.

Early in August 1962, the British and Malayan Governments

decided that the proposed Federation of Malaysia should be brought into being by 31 August 1963. After the transfer of sovereignty (Mr Sandys, the Colonial Secretary, said in announcing the Federation) there would be a transition period during which a number of constitutional powers would be delegated temporarily to the State Governments.

Hitherto opposition to the proposals for the Federation of Malaysia had taken a peaceful form, but on 8 December 1962, an organization calling itself the Borneo National Army staged a revolt, occupied the oil-centre at Seria in Brunei, attacked the sultan's palace un-successfully, and captured as hostages a number of Brunei Shell Oil Company employees. It was at once made clear that the Brunei left-wing Peoples' Party (Party Ra'ayat) whose members occupied the seats filled by election to the Legislative Council, was behind the outbreak. The Party's leader, S. M. Azahari, simultaneously issued a statement from Manila where he claimed to be on his way to the U.S.A. to put his party's case before the United Nations. British and Ghurka troops and units of the R.A.F. with naval support were quickly dispatched to Brunei. Seria was freed of rebels on 9 December though the clearing of the airfield itself was not achieved until the 12th. By Sunday, 16 December, the revolt was over.

In the House of Representatives in Kuala Lumpur on 11 Decem-ber, the Prime Minister, Tunku Abdul Rahman, said that Azahari wanted to bring the three territories of Brunei, Sarawak, and North Borneo under foreign rule. Azahari had close connections with the leaders of the Socialist Front in the Federation and with Barisan Socialis in Singapore. It was alleged that the revolting troops had been trained and armed in Indonesian Borneo.

The hostility of President Sukarno of Indonesia to the creation of Malaysia was now undisguised. In spite of a meeting in July 1963 in Manila between Tunku Abdul Rahman, President Sukarno, and President Macapagal of the Philippines when there was talk of an agreement to form an even larger federation of Maphilindo (Malaya/Philippines/Indonesia), President Sukarno increasingly opposed the establishment of Malaysia. When the Cobbold Com-mission reported that the peoples of Sarawak and Sabah favoured joining Malaysia, which was confirmed by the respective legislatures, he objected that their views had not been properly ascertained. To meet this objection, the Malaya and Singapore leaders, with the concurrence of the British Government, agreed that the declaration of Malaysia should be delayed to allow United Nations representatives to visit Sarawak and Sabah to ascertain whether the legislatures had properly consulted public opinion. The United Nations delegation which then visited the territories reported that this had been done and that popular opinion favoured the creation of the Federation. On 16 September Malaysia was proclaimed.

In 1964, the success of Malaysia seemed to depend internally on the maintenance of the power of the Alliance Party in the Federation of Malaya and the extension of the 'Alliance' idea to Sarawak and Sabah. The resounding victory won by the Alliance Party in the Malayan elections of April 1964, together with 36 seats which the Tunku already possessed in Sarawak and Sabah, gave him 125 seats in the 159-member Malaysian Federal Parliament. Meanwhile, the PAP had more than re-established its position in Singapore in the elections of September 1963, when Mr Lee Kuan-Yew had won a victory of 37 out of 51 seats.

But Indonesian reaction to the proclamation of Malaysia was violent. Mobs in Jakarta sacked the British embassy. The Indonesian Government refused to recognize Malaysia. The sequel was the breaking off by Malaysia of diplomatic relations with both Indonesia and the Philippines. Indonesia also suspended trade with Malaysia and this caused Singapore a 9 per cent loss of national income and considerable unemployment. Along the 980-mile frontier of Sarawak and Sabah Indonesian guerrilla harassment began, taking the form of raids on villages and ambushing of security forces. Then (in December 1963) Mr Robert Kennedy, the US Attorney-General, took the initiative with an attempt at mediation. At the end of January 1964 there was an Indonesian cease-fire declaration; and in February and March the Foreign Ministers of Indonesia, Malaysia and the Philippines met in Bangkok and reached broad agreement that the Siamese should supervise a cease-fire in Borneo. But the talks broke down in March. The Filippino mediator, Dr Salvador

Lopez, then succeeded in arranging a meeting of the three Foreign Ministers in Tokio on 18 June on the understanding that it should coincide with a withdrawal of Indonesian forces from Malaysian Borneo. A summit meeting followed, but failed to reach agreement on any of the points at issue between Malaysia and Indonesia. There was, however, a declaration in favour of the setting up of an Afro-Asian Consultative Commission to examine the quarrel.

The breakdown of the talks had been on the issue of whether Indonesia should cease hostilities before a political settlement was reached. Indonesia continued to insist that further withdrawals of Indonesian forces from Malaysia should be geared to the progress of political talks. The political aims of President Sukarno appeared to be to get Malaysia to sever her special relationship with Britain, and to secure some fresh consultation of the wishes of the Sarawak and Sabah peoples over the issue of joining Malaysia.

On 17 August 1964 Indonesian aggressiveness took a new turn. Indonesian forces landed on the coast of Johore. On 2 September there was a second landing – airborne – of about 100 Indonesian troops. Neither of these raids had any military effect and most of the raiders were rounded up or surrendered. But in the same month Malaysia took the issue to the United Nations Security Council. The upshot was a moral victory for Malaysia. Nine of the eleven members of the Security Council voted for a Norwegian resolution deploring the landing of Indonesian parachutists. Only the Soviet veto prevented this resolution's adoption. There were, however, further Indonesian sea-landings in Malaysia during October and December although President Sukarno agreed (20 September) to mediation in the Malaysian dispute by President Ayub of Pakistan. On 7 January 1965 the Indonesian President, obviously discom-fited by the UN resolution of the previous September, and objecting to the accession of Malaysia as a member of the Security Council, withdrew his country from United Nations membership.

The military results of Indonesian confrontation appeared to be negligible. True, Malaysia's own armed forces could not alone have repulsed, or even contained, Indonesian attacks. But under the Defence Treaties of 1957 and 1963, British, Australian and New

Zealand forces were stationed in Malaya and at the Singapore base. British units were at once deployed along the harassed borders of Sabah and Sarawak. Several waves of reinforcements were des﹆patched from Britain between 1963 and 1965 so that by January of the latter year there were about 50,000 Commonwealth troops in Malaysia. Naval forces, which included two aircraft carriers, a guided missile destroyer and three squadrons of frigates, were in action to prevent Indonesian sea﹆landings in Malaya.

But if Indonesian military operations were unimpressive in them﹆selves there was some evidence that confrontation increased racial and political tension inside Malaysia itself.

In general the tension between Singapore and Malaya mirrored the Malays' fears of the 'go ahead' Chinese in their midst, and it played into the hands of Malay racial extremists. In July and September 1964 there were serious race riots in Singapore with some thirty deaths and many hundred injured. The Malaysian Government claimed to have evidence that Indonesian agents had provoked and exacerbated the September riots. A dramatic develop﹆ment took place in January 1965 when a number of Malay leaders were placed in detention on the grounds that they had been involved in an Indonesian plot to begin an armed revolution. It seemed clear that President Sukarno's primary aim was to achieve the political disintegration of Malaysia by appealing to Malay racial feeling and to Pan﹆Malaysian sentiments which aspired to unite Malaysia with the Indonesian Republic.

But it was deeply﹆rooted animosities within Malaysia itself, which were to split the Federation. Relations between Chinese populated Singapore, with its modern﹆minded, socialistic ruling People's Action Party (PAP) and the conservative Malay﹆led alliance of Tunku Abdul Rahman in Malaya had always been difficult. There had been acrimonious bargaining in 1963 to ensure that pro﹆vision for a Malaysian Common Market, essential for Singapore's industrialization, should be incorporated in the new federal con﹆stitution. There were differences, too, over Tunku Abdul Rahman's foreign policy for Malaysia which Mr Lee Kuan﹆Yew, the Singapore Premier, considered put too much accent on crude anti﹆communism and too little on the enlistment of the sympathy of the Afro-Asian world for Malaysia's cause. But what angered the Malay-led alliance more than anything else was Lee Kuan-Yew's decision to run People's Action Party candidates in the mainland Malayan elections of April 1964. This was a PAP challenge to the Chinese capitalist component of the mainland Alliance which Lee hoped to supplant in order to take his own socialist PAP into political partnership with the Malays at the Federal Centre. But the move brought the Malays into the fray on the side of the Alliance Chinese, particularly as Tunku Abdul Rahman's prior agreement had not been obtained. All but one of the nine PAP candidates were defeated.

During the next fifteen months relations between Singapore and Kuala Lumpur steadily and disastrously deteriorated. In November 1964 new Federal turnover and payroll taxes enacted by the Malaysian Government were attacked in Singapore as a blow against its Chinese mercantile community. And in February 1965 the Deputy Premier of Singapore accused Kuala Lumpur of treating the island as 'a minor state'. Soon afterwards an acrimonious dispute about Singapore's share of Malaysian textile exports to Britain, under a new British quota offer, came to a head. The Singapore Finance Minister protested against the allotment by the Central government of an unfairly large amount of this quota to the Malayan mainland. He complained that Singapore was being considered by Kuala Lumpur not as a component State of Malaysia but as a dangerous rival to be kept down.

By April it had become clear that the mainland Malay leaders resented what they were convinced was Lee Kuan-Yew's intention to play a leading part in the Federal government of Malaysia. Tunku Abdul Rahman declared that Singapore should be content with being the 'New York of Malaysia', and that Lee should not aspire to a share in running the Federation. A few weeks later the Malaysian Vice-Premier Tun Razak urged Singapore to 'find another leader'; and the situation worsened very sharply when Lee Kuan-Yew announced the calling of a Solidarity Convention of Malaysian parties opposed to the Alliance. The Secretary-General of the United Malays National Association (UMNO) urged the

Kuala Lumpur government to act against the Singapore Prime Minister on the ground that he was stirring up ill-will between the races; and also accused him of trying to end Malay constitutional privileges. After a visit by Lee Kuan-Yew to Australia and New Zealand the U M N O Secretary-General attacked him for attempting to alienate opinion, in those countries, from the Malaysian leadership.

On 9 August 1965 Singapore was virtually expelled from the Malaysian Federation. The agreement under which the separation took place recognized the independence and sovereignty of Singapore. But it envisaged a Malaysia-Singapore Defence Treaty under which a joint defence council was to be formed; Malaysia was to provide defence aid for Singapore; Singapore was to allow Malaysia to continue to have, and make use of, bases in Singapore; and the two states were to co-operate in economic affairs, and to set up joint committees for that purpose.

The months following the breach saw efforts – not very success-ful ones – to implement the *modus vivendi* between Singapore and truncated Malaysia. Mutual antipathy continued to be both economic: Kuala Lumpur's fear of Singapore's industrial pro-ficiency, and racial: Malay distrust of the thrustful Singapore Chinese. Trade restrictions were introduced immediately after the split. But two months later they were lifted. On 18 August a Singapore-Malaysia Joint Defence Council was formed. By March 1966, however, Singapore had left the new Council. There had been differences about the stationing of a Malay battalion on the island. *Ad hoc* joint defence arrangements were then made. Soon after the split the legality of Lee Kuan-Yew's People's Action Party branches in Malaysia were successfully challenged (though they were later allowed to operate under the changed name of Democratic Action Party). The Malaysian Government protested against 'disparaging remarks' by Lee Kuan-Yew in television and press interviews.

A main focus of tension from October 1965 onwards was the Singapore government's plan to resume trade with Indonesia. But the Singapore-Malaysia split in August 1965 had been followed by decisively important events in Indonesia. President Sukarno's domestic position was crucially weakened, in October, by the abortive Communist coup in Jakarta. This caused an immediate slackening of Indonesian confrontation of Malaysia. On 11 August 1966 confrontation was formally ended by agreements, signed in Jakarta, between Malaysia and the new leadership of Indonesia. They restored peaceful relations, and Malaysia agreed to give the people of the Borneo states an opportunity to reaffirm, through general elections, as soon as practicable, their previous decision about their status in the Federation. Several months earlier a delegation of the Indonesian 'Crush Malaysia' Command had told the Malaysian Premier in Kuala Lumpur that, notwithstanding what President Sukarno might say, they had decided to call off confrontation. In June 1966, therefore, Tunku Abdul Rahman had actually welcomed Indonesian diplomatic recognition of Singapore; and a few days later the Malaysian and Singapore Premiers met and agreed 'to co-operate, maintain close relations, and not interfere in each other's domestic affairs'. But co-operation – particularly in the economic and defence fields – continued to prove elusive. On 18 August 1966 it was announced that Malaysia and Singapore would have separate currencies from June 1967.

The secession of Singapore from Malaysia had reverberations in the two Borneo territories, Sabah and Sarawak. Both of them, with their large non-Malay majorities, had valued Singapore's membership as a counterweight to the power and numbers of the Malays of the mainland, in the new Federation. Left alone with Malaya the Borneo tribal peoples' fear of Malay domination reasserted itself. In August 1965 Mr Donald Stephens, the Federal Minister for Sabah Affairs whose Kadazan Party (UPKO) had asked for a review of Sabah's position in the Federation, got a negative response from Kuala Lumpur about this. He resigned, and later retired from politics. But months earlier Kadazan-Malay tension had become evident, inside Sabah, when Stephens as Chief Minister clashed with the Head of State, Dato Mustapha, the Malay leader of USNO, the party of the Muslim peoples of Sabah. What the Kadazans particularly feared was the replacement of the outgoing British colonial officials by Malays from the mainland.

In Sarawak the non-Malay tribal peoples harboured similar

fears; they also suspected that Malay might be imposed on them as the national language in 1967. Tension between Sarawak and Kuala Lumpur was accentuated by the strong political conscious, ness of Sarawak's 30 per cent of Chinese and by the fact that the preponderantly Chinese Sarawak United People's Party (SUPP) was infiltrated by the Clandestine Communist Organization whose intimidatory activities made necessary the compulsory resettlement (in 1965) of several thousand Chinese farmers in areas of Sarawak where they would be less vulnerable to communist pressure. The fragmentation of native Dayaks and Malays – into four political parties – added to Sarawak's instability. Although all the parties, except the SUPP, had by 1963 combined together in an Alliance on the model of the mainland Malayan one, with which they joined to form the Malaysian Alliance, Sarawak's instability became manifest in 1966 when the Dayak Chief Minister, Dato Stephen Ningkan (leader of the Sarawak National Party), got at logger, heads with Kuala Lumpur, and was made to quit office through combined Alliance pressure. The evident causes of disagreement were Ningkan's desire that British troops and officials should stay in Sarawak, and mainland suspicions that he was angling for SUPP support in his differences with Kuala Lumpur. In Septem, ber 1966 the Federal government detailed a State of Emergency in Sarawak. Dato Ningkan was replaced as Sarawak Premier by Penghulu Tawi Sli, the Malaysian Federal government's nominee for the post. These events seemed to make clear that one essential condition for consolidating the Borneo territories within Malaysia would be the more rapid training of local Sarawak and Sabah people to enable them to take over the administration of their own territories.

The other piece in the jigsaw puzzle of truncated Malaysia, the tiny but oil,rich Brunei Sultanate, had in 1963 declined to join Malaysia because the Kuala Lumpur leaders had insisted on a 40 per cent contribution of Brunei's large oil reserves to the Federal treasury. Brunei, therefore, remained a protectorate of Britain which continued to station forces in the Sultanate. Political conditions in Brunei had gradually become more settled, after the suppression of the 1962 rebellion, and – although there were arrests in February 1965 – elections took place, in the following month, for ten out of the twenty-one seats in the legislative council. Four out of the ten elected members had taken part in the 1962 rebellion. In August 1965 the Brunei Sultan reiterated that he had no intention either of joining Malaysia or taking his kingdom into a possible Federation of the North Borneo States. Brunei was thus at the end of 1966 one of the several remaining tiny enclaves of the colonial empire of which Britain found it difficult to divest herself. One illogicality of the situation was the fact that Brunei's great wealth from oil was far in excess of what was needed for its own development, and would have been of the greatest value in the economic development of Malaysia as a whole.

Britain's relations with the severed parts of Malaysia after 1965 were naturally difficult and delicate. The Malaysian-British Defence Treaty remained in operation, but defence arrangements with Singapore were, after August 1965, virtually on an *ad hoc* basis, the British still provided a quarter of Singapore's income and directly employed more than 30,000 workers. The British Government wanted the Malaysia-Singapore Defence Treaty provided for in 1965, to be made a reality so as to facilitate new British-Singapore defence accords. But Lee Kuan-Yew declined to finalize the treaty until the other part of the separation agreement of 1965 – provided for economic co-operation with Malaysia – should have been implemented. In the light of the uncertain relations between Malaysia and Singapore, Britain in May 1966 declined to grant increased military aid to Malaysia. The Malaysian Government wanted about £75 million of additional British defence grants for its 1966–70 Five Year Plan. But Britain, while continuing existing aid, refused that request. Malaysian Ministers spoke of reviewing their country's relations with Britain. In August 1966 Commonwealth preferences on one-fifth of British exports to Malaysia were abolished. In September in the light of Indonesia's ending of confrontation, it was announced that all British forces would leave Borneo at the beginning of 1967. Meanwhile Kuala Lumpur stated that the Malaysian Army would be doubled.

Malaysia in 1966 consisted of an uneasy 'rump' of the original Federation. The primary reason for the two Borneo States to be inside it – in order to counterbalance Singapore's 1½ million Chinese – had gone with Singapore's departure. But, partly as a matter of prestige, Kuala Lumpur was anxious to maintain Malaysia; and in the first Malaysian Economic Plan (for 1966–70) about 16 per cent of the public investment was in Sarawak and Sabah. Singapore, outside the Federation, was bound to be seen as an unsettling element by Kuala Lumpur. Singapore's interest in finding markets and outlets for its growing population in the Borneo territories inevitably generated Malay fears that Lee Kuan-Yew intended ultimately to detach Sabah and Sarawak from Malaysia. But it was hard to distinguish cause from effect: Singapore resented what it considered the Malaysian Government's failure to implement economic co-operation. Because of economic pressures the island urgently needed access to the Malaysian market – to make possible industrialization and the employment of its steadily increasing, predominantly youthful, population.

Soon after separation the Singapore government restricted the employment of non-Singaporeans, including Malaysians, and denied them free educational facilities. In 1965 unemployment in Singapore was increased at an annual rate of 10,000. Sixty per cent of Singaporeans in 1966 were under twenty-one. Endeavours to attract foreign industrial investment were failing to reach their targets because of uncertainty as to the island's access to external markets. Yet Kuala Lumpur's policy appeared to be to compete with, rather than complement, Singapore's industrial development. And, in the field of trade the Malaysian Government was doing its utmost to develop Port Swettenham and Penang, apparently to replace Singapore, as ports for servicing Malaysia's large export and import trade: a serious matter for Singapore, 30 per cent of whose trade was, in normal times, with Malaysia. At the same time the ending of confrontation did not at once bring back Singapore's full normal volume of trade with Indonesia. Anti-Chinese feeling in Indonesia tended towards a cooling-off of relations with Chinese traders in Singapore.

One possibility that was conjured up in 1966 was of some kind of concerted Malaysian-Indonesian action, based on Pan-Malay anti-Chinese feeling, and aimed at 'bringing Singapore to heel'. Such speculation, was, however, based on over-simplification. Malaysia, in the long run, could ill afford to dispense with the skills of Singapore, and she needed the wider market for her products which a Malaysian-Singapore Common Market could provide. It was moreover in the long-term interest of the entire region of South-east Asia that international rivalries and disputes should be replaced by a growing-together of the peoples. There appeared to be no sane way to create a balance between China and her neighbours except by the development of co-operation and stable, harmonious groupings among the smaller nations on China's perimeter. In 1961 the Association of Southeast Asia (A S A), a loose consultative group of Malaysia, Thailand and the Philippines had been set up. It ceased to function in 1963 when the Filippinos refused to recognize Malaysia. But in 1966 A S A was reactivated, and at a meeting in Bangkok its members agreed to attempt co-operation in higher education, the formation of a shipping-line and the liberalization of trade. Singapore, significantly and regrettably, did not attend. It had moreover become evident that any Southeast Asian grouping which aspired to wield strong political influence must include Indonesia. There was talk of reviving and enlarging the Maphilindo idea. Maphilindo was originally to include Indonesia but not Thailand. It certainly appeared at the end of 1966 that – following the restoration of peace between Indonesia and Malaysia – what was most needed was an end to the smaller, but nonetheless damaging, confrontation between Malaysia and Singapore.

Notes on the text

1 MALAYA: ROOTS IN THE PAST

1 De Eredia (1613) says 1398.
2 A detailed sociological account of traditional, pre-intervention Malay society is to be found in J. M. Gullick, *Indigenous Political Systems of Western Malaya*, University of London, Athlone Press, 1958.

2 THE PEOPLE OF MALAYA

3 The end-year estimate for 1962 was 7,491,325.
4 See *Statesman's Year Book*, 1962, and for other years. The estimates for mid-1961 were 3,576,889 Malaysians, 2,633,516 Chinese, 796,880 Indians and Pakistanis, and 129,519 others.
5 *ibid.*, regarding 'Malaysia' and 'Malaysians' see Note on p. 12.
6 Alastair Lamb, *Chandi Bukit Batu Pahat*, Singapore, 1960.
7 For a detailed description of the shadow-play, see Sir Richard Winstedt, *The Malays, a Cultural History*, Kegan Paul, 1950, pp. 29, 30.

3 THE AGE OF IMPERIALISM

8 The Yang di-Pertuan Agong, or King, was elected by the Rulers of the Malay States after independence in 1957.
9 An excellent general account of the period is in J. Kennedy, *A History of Malaya A.D. 1400–1959*, London, Macmillan, 1962, Chapter 9. More detailed accounts of British intervention are C. N. Parkinson, *British Intervention in Malaya 1867–1877*, University of Malaya Press, 1960, and C. D. Cowan, *Nineteenth Century Malaya*, Oxford University Press, 1961.

211

10 An account critical of the British but giving them credit for their positive achievements is R. Emerson, *Malaysia, A Study in Direct and Indirect Rule*, New York, 1937. Emerson, Professor of Government at Harvard, compares British rule in Malaya with Dutch rule in Indonesia.

11 John Crawfurd, F.R.S., *A Descriptive Dictionary of the Indian Islands and the Adjacent Countries*, London, 1856, p. 66.

12 *Sarawak: Report for the year 1962*, London, HMSO, 1963.

13 *North Borneo Annual Report, 1962*, London, HMSO, 1963.

14 K. G. Tregonning, *Under Chartered Company Rule (North Borneo 1881–1946)*, Singapore, 1958, p. 4.

15 *ibid.*

16 For fuller details, see T. E. Smith, *The Background to Malaysia*, September 1963 (Chatham House Memoranda).

Abbreviations

AMCJA	All-Malayan Council of Joint Action
API	Angkatan Permuda Insaf (Youth Party)
ASA	Association of Southeast Asia
BARJASA	Barisan Anak Jati Sarawak Party
FMS	Federated Malay States (British Period)
IMP	Independence of Malaya Party
KMT	Kuomintang (Chinese Nationalist Party)
MCA	Malayan Chinese Association
MCP	Malayan Communist Party
MCS	Malayan Civil Service (British)
MDU	Malayan Democratic Union
MIC	Malayan Indian Congress
MNP	Malayan Nationalist Party
MPAJA	Malayan People's Anti-Japanese Army
MPLA	Malayan People's Liberation Army
PANAS	Party Negara Sarawak
PAP	People's Action Party
PMIP	Pan Malayan Islamic Party
PPP	People's Progressive Party
PUTERA	Pusat Tenaga Ra'ayat (People's United Front)
SEATO	Southeast Asia Treaty Organization
SNP	Sarawak National Party
SUPP	Sarawak United People's Party
UDP	United Democratic Party
UMNO	United Malay National Organization

Select Bibliography

JMBRAS=Journal of the Malayan Branch, Royal Asiatic Society

Abdullah bin Abdul Kadir, *Pelayaran Abdullah* (trans. by A. E. Coope), Singapore, 1949

Allen, G. C., and Donnithorne, A. C., *Western Enterprise in Indonesia and Malaya*, 1957

Bauer, P. T., *The Rubber Industry*, 1948

Blythe, W., 'Historical Sketch of Chinese Labour in Malaya', *JMBRAS*, xx, 1, 1947

Brown, C. C., *Malay Annals* (translation), *JMBRAS*, xxv, 2, 3, 1952

Buckley, C. B., *An Anecdotal History of Old Times in Singapore (1819–1867)*, 1902

Burkhill, I., *A Dictionary of Economic Products of the Malay Peninsula*, 2 vols., 1935

Chapman, F. Spencer, *The Jungle is Neutral*, 1949

Cheeseman, H. R., *Bibliography of Malaya*, 1959

Chin Kee Onn, *Malaya Upside Down*, Singapore, 1946
Ma-ri-ee, 1952

Clodd, H. P., *Malaya's First British Pioneer (Francis Light)*, 1948

Cobbold Report on Sarawak and North Borneo, 1962

Comber, Leon, *Secret Societies in Malaya*, Singapore, 1957

Cowan, C. D., *Nineteenth Century Malaya, The Origins of British Political Control*, 1961

Dobby, E. H. G., *South-East Asia*, 1957

Emerson, Rupert, *Malaysia, A Study in Direct and Indirect Rule*, New York, 1937
Representative Government in Southeast Asia, Harvard, 1955

Fermor, L., *Report upon the Mining Industry of Malaya*, Kuala Lumpur, 1939

Ginsburg, N., and Roberts, C. F., *Malaya*, Seattle, 1958

Gullick, J. M., *Indigenous Political Systems of Western Malaya*, 1956
'Kuala Lumpur 1880–1895', *JMBRAS*, xxviii, 4, 1955
Malaya (Nations of the Modern World), 1963

Wang Gungwu, *A Short History of the Nanyang Chinese*, Singapore, 1959

Hahn, Emily, *Raffles of Singapore*, 1948

Hall, D. G. E., *A History of South-East Asia*, 1955

Harrison, B., *A Short History of South-East Asia*, 1954

Hobbs, Cecil, *Southeast Asia: an annotated bibliography of selected reference sources*, Washington, 1952

Jones, S. W., *Public Administration in Malaya*, 1952

Kennedy, J., *A History of Malaya, A.D. 1400–1959*, 1962

Lamb, Alastair, *Chandi Bukit Batu Pahat*, Singapore, 1960 (Archaeology of Malaya)

Linehan, W., 'A History of Pahang', *JMBRAS*, xiv, 2, 1936

Maxwell, W. G., and Gibson, W. S., *Treaties and Engagements affecting the Malay States and Borneo*, 1924

Middlebrook, S. M., 'Yap Ah Loy', *JMBRAS*, xxiv, 2, 1951

Mills, L. A., *British Malaya, 1824–1867*, Singapore, 1925

Newbold, T., *Political and Statistical Account of the British Settlements in the Straits of Malacca*, 2 vols., 1839

Parkinson, C. Northcote, *British Intervention in Malaya, 1867–1877*, Singapore, 1960

Pelzer, Karl J., *Selected Bibliography on the Geography of Southern Asia, Pt. III, Malaya*, New Haven, 1956

Pires, Tomé, *Suma Oriental (1512–1515)* (trans. by A. Cortesao) (Hakluyt Society), 2 vols., 1944

Purcell, Victor, *The Chinese in Southeast Asia* (revd. ed.), 1963
The Revolution in Southeast Asia, 1962
Malaya, Communist or Free?, 1954
The Chinese in Malaya, 1948

Robequain, C., *Malaya, Indonesia, Borneo and the Philippines* (trans. by E. D. Laborde), 1955

Runciman, Steven, *The White Rajahs*, 1962

Silcock, T. H., *The Economy of Malaya*, Singapore, 1956

Smith, T. E., *Population Growth in Malaya*, 1952
Malaysia (Chatham House Memoranda), 1963

Straits Times Annual (for colour reproductions of Malayan art and archaeology)

Swettenham, Sir Frank, *British Malaya*, 1948
Footprints in Malaya, 1943

Tarling, N., *Anglo-Dutch Rivalry in the Malay World, 1780–1824*, 1962
'British Policy in the Malay Peninsula and Archipelago', *JMBRAS*, xxx, 3, 1957

Tregonning, K. G., *Under Chartered Company Rule: North Borneo, 1881–1946*
Wallace, A. Russel, *The Malay Archipelago*, 1869
Who's Who, Leaders of Malaya, Kuala Lumpur, 1957–8, ed. by J. Victor Morais
Winstedt, Sir R. O., *A History of Malaya* (revd. ed.), Singapore, 1962
  Malaya and its History, 1951
  The Malays. A Cultural History, 1950
  'A History of Selangor', *JMBRAS*, XII, 3, 1934
  'A History of Perak' (with R. J. Wilkinson), *JMBRAS*, XII, 1, 1934
  'A History of Johore', *JMBRAS*, X, 3, 1932
Wurtzburg, C. E., *Raffles of the Eastern Isles*, 1954
Year-Books (official) of Malaya, Singapore, Sarawak, and North Borneo (Sabah)

Acknowledgements

Associated Press, 70, 76; British Overseas Airways Corporation, 32; Miss N. Baker, 62; The Borneo Company, 40, 90; from Sir J. Brooke, *Borneo and the Celebes*, 1848, 84; J. Allen Cash, 82; Camera Press, 17, 21, 25, 29, 51 (John Bulmer), 56, 75, 80, 81; Central Press Photos, 72; from F. Cuesta, *Nuevo Viagero Universal*, 1859–62, by courtesy of the Trustees of the British Museum, 86, 87; Dunlop Rubber Co, 20, 44, 58, 59; from G. de Eredia, *Malaca, l'Inde Meridionale et le Cathay*, 1613 (edition of 1882), by courtesy of the Trustees of the British Museum, 4, 5, 6, 8; Government Archives, Malaya, 41; *Illustrated London News*, 35; *Journal of the Malayan Branch of the Royal Asiatic Society*, 3; Keystone Press Agency, 31, 63, 68, 71, 73, 79, 97; Malaysia House, London, 11, 14, 16, 19, 22, 23, 24, 28, 30, 36, 39, 43, 50, 52, 65, 66, 78; Malayan Rubber Co Ltd London, 55, 57; Ministry of Culture, Singapore (Sarawak Information Service and Sabah Director of Information), 96, 98; from Capt Mundy and Sir J. Brooke, *Narrative of Events in Borneo and the Celebes down to the Occupation of Labuan*, 1848, 88; National Museum, Kuala Lumpur, 1; National Portrait Gallery, London, 83; from J. Pontanus, *Rerum et Urbis Amsteldameensium Historia*, 1611, 2, 9; J. Pope-Hennessy, 10, 13, 38; Paul Popper Limited, 74, 77; Radio Times Hulton Picture Library, 12, 46, 64, 67, 69; P. A. Reuter Photos, 26, 42, 91, 93, 94; M. Rawstorne, 89, 92; W. Suschitzky, 15, 18, 45; Singapore National Museum, 27, 33, 34; Shell Co Ltd, 95; from J. A. St John, *Views of the Eastern Archipelago*, 1847, by courtesy of the Trustees of the British Museum, 85; Tin Industry Board, Ipoh, Perak, 53, 54; Ure-Smith Pty, Australia, 60, 61; G. H. Wood, 37, 47, 48, 49.

216

Who's Who

Abang Haji Mustapha bin Abang Haji Moasili, C.B.E. (1906–64), Datu Bandar of Sarawak. Chairman of Party Negara Sarawak (Panas). Signatory of the London Agreement on Malaysia.

Abdul Aziz bin Ishak, Enche. b. 1914. Ed. Malay Schools, Kuala Kurau and Taiping, Victoria Bridge School, and Raffles Institution: Singapore Fisheries Officer: 1946–8 President Gerakan Angkatan Pemuda Melayu (Malay Youth Action League): Minister of Agriculture and Co-operatives, Federation of Malaya until 1963 (resigned).

Abdul Hamid Khan bin Haji Sakhawat Ali, J.M.N., b. 1900. Trained as teacher. Minister of Welfare Services, Malaysia, 1964.

Abdul Rahman, Wan, bin Datu Tuanku Bujang. b. Sibu, 1925. Ed. Sibu Malay School, St Thomas's School. Member of Federal House of Representatives (Malaysian Parliament). Member of Barisan Raayat Jati Sarawak. Labour Dept., Kuala Belait, 1956–7.

Abdul Rahman, Y.T.M. Tunku Abdul Rahman Putra Al-Haj ibni Almarhum Sultan Abdul Hamid Halim Shah, K.O.M., C.H., b. 1902. Ed. Malaya and St Catharine's College, Cambridge. B.A., Hon. LL.D. President of UMNO. Prime Minister of Malaysia, Minister of External Affairs, 1964.

Abdul Rahman bin Haji Talib, Enche. b. 1916. Ed. Malay and English schools, Pahang. Minister of Transport, Minister of Education, Malaysia, 1964.

Abdul Razak, Tun Haji Razak bin Dato Hussein, S.M.N., b. 1922, Pekan. Ed. Malay College, Kuala Kangsar. Barrister-at-Law, Lincoln's Inn. Deputy Prime Minister, Minister of Defence, National and Rural Development, Lands and Mines, Malaysia, 1964.

Abdul Taib bin Mahmud. Member of Supreme Council, Sarawak. b. 1936.

Ed. St Joseph's School, Kuching, University of Adelaide, Australia. Bachelor of Law. Barrister and Solicitor of Supreme Court of Australia. Legal Cadet, Sarawak Govt. 1962–3.

Abdullah, Munshi, Raffles' Malay teacher, author of *Hikayat Abdullah*.

Abdullah, Sultan of Perak, banished to Seychelles, 1875.

Abdur Rahman, last Emperor of Johore, d. 1830.

Albuquerque, Alfonso d' (1452–1515). Portuguese Governor of the Indies, conquered Malacca (1511).

Ahmad bin Mohammed Ibrahim, Queen's Scholar, 1935. Ed. Raffles College, University of London (B.A.) and St John's College, Cambridge (First Class in Economics, Tripos Part I and Law Part II). Minister of Labour, Singapore.

Bahaman bin Samsudin, Enche, b. 1906. Ed. St Paul's Institution, Seremban, and Malay College, Kuala Kangsar. MCS 1937. Minister of Health, Malaysia, 1964.

Banyang anak P. Janting, Pengavah, b. Julan, Sarawak, 1914. Ed. Julan School. Member of Federal House of Representatives (Malaysian Parliament). Member of Council Nigri. Chairman, Party Pesaka anak Sarawak.

Barker, E. W., b. 1922. Speaker of Singapore Legislative Assembly. Barrister (Inner Temple). M.A., LL.B. (St Catharine's College, Cambridge).

Braga, Armand Joseph, b. 1900. Ed. Christian Brothers School of Singapore and Queen's College, Hong Kong. Called to Bar by Middle Temple, 1927. Advocate and solicitor. Late Minister of Health, Singapore.

Brooke, Sir Charles Anthony Johnson (1829–1917). Second 'White Raja' of Sarawak.

Brooke, Sir Charles Vyner (1874–1964). Third and last 'White Raja' of Sarawak.

Brooke, Sir James (1803–68). First 'White Raja' of Sarawak.

Burhanuddin, Dr, b. 1911. Ed. Malay School, Kota Bharu, Arabic and English School, teacher, merchant, journalist. Ex-President Malay Nationalist Party (MNP). President Pan-Malayan Islamic Party (PMIP).

Byrne, K. M., b. 1915. Ed. St Joseph's Institution and Raffles College. Colonial Administrative Service, 1946. Minister of Health and Law, Singapore.

Cheng Ho (d. *c.* 1431). Chief of the Chinese eunuch admirals who visited Malaysia between 1405 and 1431.

Chew Swee Kee, b. 1918. Ed. Chung Wah Chinese School, Ipoh. Chinese Secretariat, courts interpreter. Minister of Education, Federation of Malaya, 1957– .

Clarke, Sir Andrew (1824–1902), Governor of the Straits Settlements who negotiated Pangkor Engagement, January 1874.

Clifford, Sir Hugh (1866–1941), negotiated treaty of protection with Pahang (1888), Governor of Straits Settlements (1827–9).

Datu Abang Haji bin Abang Sapi,ee, O.B.E. Governor of Sarawak. b. Kuching 1902, Ed. Govt. School, St Anthony's School, Sarikei, St Thomas's Night School. Joined Govt. in 1924. President of Majlis Islam Sarawak, 1955–63.

Datu Mustapha bin Harum, O.B.E., Head of State, Orang Kaya. A Sulu, b. in Kudat, about 1914. Son of a Malay Chief in Kudat District and succeeded father as senior native chief. A Muslim native tongue Suluk, but speaks Malay fluently. Guerilla leader during Japanese occupation. Sabah Legislative and Executive Councils, 1953. An early supporter of Malaysia.

Datu Temenggong Juga, Minister for Sarawak Affairs, Malaysia, 1964.

Datu Tuanku Bujang bin Tuanku Osmam, O.B.E. Ed. Malay School, Sibu. Federal Senator. Founder and leader of Barisan Raayat Jati Sarawak (Barjasa), b. Sibu 1898.

Devaser, Kimden Lal, B.A. (London), b. India (Punjab) 1912. Lawyer. President MIC (1951–5).

Enchana, Dunstan Endawi anak. State Minister for Local Govt., b. Saratok, 1937. Ed. St Peter's School, Suratok and St Augustine's School, Betong. Schoolteacher, then farmer. Member of Sarawak National Party.

Fa Hsien, Chinese Buddhist pilgrim, visited Malaysia 1413 on his way back from India to China.

Fong Swee Suan, Organizing Secretary of Barisan Socialis.

Goh Keng Swee, Dr, Minister of Culture, and later (1963) Minister of Finance, Singapore, b. 1919. Ed. Anglo,Chinese School, Singapore, Raffles College, University of London (B.Sc., Ph.D.). In Government Service for twenty years.

Gunn Lay Teck, M.A., b. Penang, 1901. Ed. St Xavier's Institute, Penang and Peterhouse, Cambridge. High Commissioner for Malaya in Australia 1957.

Haji Mohammad bin Haji Muhammad Tahir, b. 1909. Ed. Govt. Malay School, St Thomas's School, Kuching. Member of Federal House of Representatives (Malaysian Parliament). Chairman and Founder of Raayat Secondary School. Secretary-General of Barisan Permuda Sarawak and later President. Publicity chief of Barisan Raayat Jati Sarawak.

Hussein (Tunku Long) recognized by Raffles as Sultan of Johore (1819).

Ibrahim, Sir (1873–1959) Sultan of Johore (1895–1959).

Ismail bin Dato Abdul Rahman, Dato, Dr, P.M.N., b. 1915. Ed. English College Johore Bahru and qualified in medicine, Melbourne University 1945. Previously Ambassador to U.S.A. Later Minister of Home Affairs and Justice, Malaysia, 1964.

Jek Yuen Thong, b. 1931. Ed. Chinese High School. Minister of Labour. Detained by Lim Yew Hock's Government in 1957.

Jervois, Sir William (1821–97). Governor of Straits Settlements (1875–7). Conducted Perak War (1875).

Jugah, Datu, anak Barieng, O.B.E., Q.R.I.C., b. 1903. Federal Minister for Sarawak Affairs. Paramount Chief of the Ibans in 3rd Div. of Sarawak. Appointed Penghulu of Merirai area, 1926. Appointed Temenggong, February 1955. Joined Australian forces 1945. One of the signatories of the Malaysia Agreement.

Jumabhoy Mohamed Jumabhoy, b. 1918, Bombay. Ed. Raffles Institution and YMCA School of Commerce. Merchant. Later Minister for Commerce and Industry, Singapore.

Kamil Mohamed Ariff, Sir, C.B.E., J.P., M.C.H., L.M.S., b. 1893. Ed. St Xavier's Institution, King Edward VII College of Medicine. Member, Penang Settlement Council since 1948. Commissioner Mohammedan and Hindu Endowment Boards, Chairman, Muslim Advisory Board and Muslim Orphanage, Penang.

Khaw Khai Boh, Deputy Superintendent of Police, ex Head of Special Branch, Singapore. Minister of Local Government and Housing, Malaysia, 1964.

Khoo Siak Chiew. Minister for Communications and Works, Sabah. Teochiu Chinese. b. 1919. Ed. 1925–34 at Ming Sing and St Mary's Schools, Sandakan, in both Chinese and English. Businessman and wealthy timber merchant. Chairman of Sandakan Chamber of Commerce for many years. Prominent in fostering political parties, first as Chairman of the United Party, and later as Secretary-General of the Borneo Utara National Party.

Lee, H. S., Col. Tun Sir Hau Shik Lee, S.M.N., K.B.E., J.P., b. 1901. Ed. Hong Kong University, London, St John's College, Cambridge (B.A. 1923). Minister of Transport, 1953–5, Minister of Finance 1955–9. (Federation of Malaya.) Instrumental in forming MCA–UMNO Alliance 1952.

Lee Kong Chian, Dato, b. 1894, Nan Ann, China. Ed. Tao Nan School, Singapore. Chinese University, Shanghai. Established Lee Rubber Company, 1931. Philanthropist, has donated $500,000 to University of Malaya Endowment Fund. Chancellor of the University of Singapore 1962.

Lee Kuan-Yew (Harry), b. 1923, Singapore. Ed. Raffles Institution (Anderson Scholar), Raffles College and Cambridge University (Double first in Law), Lawyer, Secretary-General, People's Action Party. (PAP) Prime Minister of Singapore 1959; re-elected, 1963.

Lee Siew Choh, Dr, Chairman of Barisan Socialis, Singapore.

Leong Yew Koh, Tun, b. 1888. Queen's Scholar, practised as lawyer. Maj.-Gen., Chinese Army, Burma, during war of 1941–5. Governor of Malacca 1957, Minister of Justice, Federation of Malaya.

Lim Kim San, Dato, b. 1918. Minister for National Development, Singapore. Ed. Anglo-Chinese School and Raffles College.

Lim Chong Eu, Dr, b. and ed. in Penang. Medical doctor. March 1958 elected President MCA, defeating incumbent President Sir Cheng Lock Tan. Resigned 1959. Founded United Democratic Party.

Lim Swee Aun, Dr, Minister of Commerce and Industry, Malaysia, 1964.

Lim Yew Hock, Tun, b. 1914. Ed. at a Chinese school for two years, then at Pearl's Hill and Outram School. Trade Union Leader. Chief Minister of Singapore, 1956– .

Loke Wan Tho, 1915–1964. Ed. Victoria Inst., Kuala Lumpur, Switzerland, King's College, Cambridge. Landowner, director of companies. Philanthropist. Gained an international reputation as an ornithologist and photographer.

Low, Sir Hugh, Resident of Perak 1877–89. Planted rubber experimentally.

Mahmud, last Sultan of Malacca, d. 1529.

Manickavasagam, Enche, V., b. 1926, Kuala Selangor. Ed. High School, Klang; Ex-President Malayan Indian Congress. Minister of Labour, Malaysia, 1964.

Marshall, David Saul, b. Singapore, 1908, of Jewish parents. Ed. Convent of Holy Infant Jesus, St Joseph's Institution, and Raffles Institution. Practised at Bar. Chief Minister of Singapore, 1955–6.

Mohamed bin Baba, succeeded Mohamed Tunku as High Commissioner for Malaya in Pakistan.

Mohamed Khir Johari, Haji, b. 1923. Ed. Sultan Abdul Hamid College, Alor Star. Formerly Gen. Sec. of SABERKAS, a Malay political body affiliated to UMNO. Sec.-Gen. UMNO, Malaya. Minister of Agriculture and Co-operatives, 1964.

Mohamed Seth bin Mohamed Said, b. 1902. Ed. Muar and Johore Bahru. Land office, Johore, aged 16. District Officer, Batu Pahat, 1950, and then State Secretary. Ambassador to Siam, 1958– .

Mohamed, Tunku, b. 1914. Ed. Malay School, Sri Menanti Malay College, Kuala Kangsar. Malayan Admin. Service, 1934. MCS, 1947. High Commissioner for Malaya in Pakistan, 1957– .

Nayaranan, P. P., b. 1923. Ed. in India and Kuala Lumpur. After liberation from Japanese organized Estate Workers' Union in Seremban which grew into Plantation Workers' Union, Malaya. Labour Leader.

Nik Ahmed Kamil, Dato, C.B.E., D.K., S.M.P.K., b. 1901, Kelantan. Ed. Majlis Ugama School, Kota Bharu, Malay College, Kuala Kangsar, Lincoln's Inn. Called to the Bar, 1930. Joined State Service of Kelantan. High Commissioner for Malaya in United Kingdom and later Ambassador to the USA and UN.

Ningkan Stephan Kalong. State Chief Minister. Secretary General to Sarawak Alliance. b. 1920. Ed. St Augustine's School, Betong. Founder and President of Dayak Association, Brunei, 1958–60. One of the prime organizers of Sarawak National Alliance.

Ong Eng-Guan, Mayor of Singapore and later PAP Minister. Resigned after disagreement with Prime Minister, Mr Lee Kuan Yew. Defeated PAP candidate at by-election, April 1961. Leader, United People's Party.

Ong Kee Hui, b. Kuching, 1914. Grandson of late Mr Ong Tiang Swee. Ed. St Thomas's School, Kuching, St Andrew's School, Singapore, College of Agriculture, Serdang, Malaya. Manager of Bian Chiang Bank. Member of Council Negri. Chairman of SUPP.

Ong Pang Boon, Minister for Home Affairs, Singapore. b. 1930. Ed. Kuala Lumpur and University of Malaya (B.A.). Organizing Secretary, PAP.

Ong Yoke Lin, Dato, PMN, b. 1918. Ed. Kuala Lumpur. Merchant and Ambassador to U.S.A. Minister without Portfolio, Malaysia, 1964.

Onn bin Ja'afar, Dato Sir (1895-1962). Son of Dato Jaafar, Mentri Besar of Johore. Ed. Malay School, Johore Bahru, Aldeburgh Lodge School, Suffolk. Government Service, Johore. Founded United Malay National Organization, 1946. Sponsored independence of Malaya Party and later Party Negara. Opposed UMNO-MCA Alliance.

Oon Beng Hong (Mrs), O.B.E., b. 1903, Penang. Ed. University of London (LL.B). Barrister (Inner Temple). Lawyer. Member Federal Council 1949-55, representing educational, professional and cultural interests.

Othman bin Mohamed, C.M.G., b. 1905, Klang. Ed. Victoria Institution, Kuala Lumpur. Joined Government Service 1925, MCS, 1935. Permanent Secretary, External Affairs Ministry, Federation of Malaya.

Othman Wok (PAP). b. 1925. Minister for Social Affairs, Singapore. Ed. Malay Schools and Raffles Institution. Journalist.

Pang Tet Tshung. Minister for Social Welfare and Education, Sabah. b. Jesselton, 1923. Ed. in Chinese at Beaufort and Jesselton, and in English at All Saints School, Jesselton. Passed Junior Cambridge examination 1939. In 1946 started Nam Kong Company with Philip Lee. 1962-3 Chairman Jesselton Chamber of Commerce. Nominated unofficial Member of Legislative Council from 1959 and Member of Executive Council from 1961.

Parameswara (Iskandar Shah) (d. 1424). First king of Malacca. Visited Peking, 1411.

Raffles, Sir T. Stamford (1781-1826). Lieut.-Gov. of Java (1811-16). Founded Singapore (1819). Co-founder of London Zoo.

Rajaratnam, Saravanamuthu, b. 1916, Ceylon. Ed. Anglo-Chinese School Perat Buntar, and High School, Bukit Mertajam. Malayan Railways. Minister of Culture, Singapore.

Sambanthan, Dato V. T., P.M.N., b. 1919. Ed. Clifford School, Kuala Kangsar, Annamalai University, S. India (B.A.). President United Indian Council, 1954. Re-elected President of MIC 1956. Minister of Works, Posts, and Communications, Malaysia, 1964.

Samsuddin, Enche Bahaman bin, b. 1906. Ed. Seremban and Malay College, Kuala Kangsar. Minister of Labour, Federation of Malaya, 1957–   .

Sardon, Dato Sardon bin Haji Jubir, P.M.N, b. 1917. Ed. Malay School, Johore, Raffles Institution, Singapore. Studied Law in England, returned 1937 and practised at S.S. and F.M.S. Bars. President of UMNO Youth since 1951 (three times). A Vice-President of UMNO, Malaya. Minister of Transport, Malaysia, 1964.

Seenivasagam Dharma Raja, b. 1921, Ipoh. Ed. Anderson School, Ipoh. Inner Temple, London. Advocate and solicitor, 1949–   . Act. Vice-President Perak Progressive Party (PPP) 1953–4. With his brother, leader of PPP in 1959 elections.

Senu Abdul Rahman, B.A., b. 1919. Ed. Sultan Idris Training College, Tanjong Malim, Los Angeles. Teacher 1939–41. Joint Secretary of the Alliance and Secretary General of UMNO, 1955–   . First Malayan Ambassador to Indonesia. Minister of Information and Broadcasting, Malaysia, 1964.

Shelley, Gilbert, O.B.E., J.P., President of Eurasian Association, 1952–   . Represented Eurasian Community in Federal Legislative Council.

Sockalingham, Dr M., C.B.E., O.S.S. Speaker of Council Negri. Private practitioner. Chairman of Sarawak Social Welfare Council. b. Telok Anson, Malaya. Ed. Anglo-Chinese School, Pioh, Perak, Methodist Boys' School, Kuala Lumpur, King Edward VII College of Medicine, Singapore. Joined National Service, 1939. Retired Member of Supreme Council, Council Negri.

Sopiee, Mohamed Sopiee bin Shaikh Ibrahim, b. 1924. Ed. St Xavier's Institution, Penang, London School of Economics. Helped to form Pan-Malayan Labour Party.

Stephens, Donald, Chief Minister, Sabah. b. Kudat, 1920. Father a clerk in the service of Chartered Company, Jules Stephens, the son of a European, the chief surveyor, by a Dusun wife. Ed. St James's School, Kudat, St Mary's, Sandakan, Government School, Kennigan, and Sacred Heart, Jesselton. A pupil teacher, then into Straits Trading Co., Singapore. Imprisoned and tortured by Japanese. Father shot by them. 1953 started *Sabah Times*. Leg. Council member, 1955. Ex. co. 1959. Played a major part in bringing together the four political parties into the Sabah Alliance Party, in 1962.

Sundang, G. S., M.B.E., Minister for Health, Sabah. b. 1909. The younger son of a distinguished Chief in Keningau. Ed. R C Mission School, Tambunan and St Thomas's School, Kuching. Joined Govt. Service, 1930. Retired District Officer, Keningau. Then succeeded brother as Native Chief, Keningau. Anti-Japanese guerilla leader, 1949-51 studied administration and local government in Europe. Nominated official member of Legislative Council from 1959.

Swettenham, Sir Frank (1850-1946), entered Straits Settlements Civil Service, 1871. Resident of Selangor 1874-5, first Resident-General, Federated Malay States, 1896, Governor, Straits Settlements, 1901-4.

Syed Ja'afar Albar, Secretary-General of UMNO (1964).

Syed Putra bin ibni Al-Marjum Syed Hassan Jamalullail, H.M. Tuanku D.M.N., S.M.N., D.K., K.C.M.G., Head of State, Malaysia, Supreme Head of State Malaya, Ruler of Perlis.

Tan, C. C. Ed. Singapore. Lawyer. Chairman of the Liberal Socialist Party. Founder member of Progressive Party, and leader of P P in former Legislative Council. President of Singapore Olympic Sports Council.

Tan Chin Tuan, C.B.E., J.P., b. 1908, Singapore. Ed. Anglo-Chinese School, Singapore. 1942 Joint Managing Director Overseas Chinese Banking Corporation, Deputy President Legislative Company, 1951-5.

Tan, Dato Sir Cheng Lock (1883-1960). Chinese leader, First President of the Malayan Chinese Association, 1949. Active in formation of M C A– U M N O Alliance.

Tan Siew Sin, Enche, J.P. Son of the late Sir Cheng Lock Tan, b. 1916. Ed. High School Malacca, and Raffles College, Singapore. Minister of Finance, Malaysia, 1964.

Tan, T. H. b. 1914, Singapore. Ed. St Joseph's Institution and Raffles College. Journalist, 1952, Chief Executive Secretary, M C A, and then Secretary Alliance Party.

Tan Tsak Yu, Member of Federal House of Representatives (Malaysian Parliament). Vice-Chairman, Sarawak Chinese Association. Vice-Chairman, Sarawak Alliance. b. China, 1903. Ed. China, Malayan Seminary, Singapore. Principal Sunny Hill School, 1931–9.

Tan, William, C.B.E., A.I.A.A. Federal Senator (nominated). Hon. Chairman Sarawak Chinese Association. b. Kuching, 1906. Ed. St Joseph's School, Kuching. Joined Sarawak PWD 1925. First President of fully-elected Kuching Municipal Council, 1956. Co-founder of Party Negara, 1960.

Teo Kui-Seng, Sarawak. State Minister for Natural Resources. Assistant Secretary General, Sarawak Chinese Association. b. Kuching, 1908. Ed. St Thomas's School and Min Teck School, Kuching, and in Singapore. Founder Member of Sarawak United Peoples' Party (SUPP), resigned November 1962.

Thuraisingham, Dato Sir Clough, b. 1898. Ed. Thomas College, Colombo, Selwyn College, Cambridge. Barrister, Middle Temple, 1924. President of Ceylon Association of Malaya.

Toh Chin Chye, Dr, Deputy Prime Minister, Singapore, b. 1921. Ed. Perak, Raffles College, Singapore, University of London (Ph.D. in Physiology). Chairman, Singapore Polytechnic.

Wee Chong Jin. b. 1917, Penang. Chief Justice of Singapore. Ed. Penang Free School. Barrister (Middle Temple) 1938. Advocate and solicitor.

Winstedt, Sir Richard, b. 1878., M.C.S. (Retd.) Malay lexicographer and historian of Malaya.

Wong Kim Meng. State Deputy. Chief Minister, Sarawak. b. 1922. Ed. St Mary's and St Thomas's Schools, Kuching. Founder of trading firm, Limbang Trading Co., 1946.

Ya'acob, Tunku. Elder brother of Tunku Abdul Rahman. Chairman of the Public Services Commission. A Pro-Chancellor of the University of Malaya. Formerly Member for Agriculture and Forestry.

Yong Nyuk Lin, b. 1918. Ed. St Paul's Institution, Seremban, Raffles College, Singapore. Assoc. Member of Chartered Insurance Institute, London. Demonstrator in Chemistry, Raffles College, 1947. Minister of Education, Singapore.

Index

229